ADVENTURE
IN Everything

Hay House Titles of Related Interest

YOU CAN HEAL YOUR LIFE, the movie, starring Louise L. Hay &
Friends (available as a 1-DVD program and an expanded 2-DVD set)
Watch the trailer at: **www.LouiseHayMovie.com**

THE SHIFT, the movie, starring Dr. Wayne W. Dyer
(available as a 1-DVD program and an expanded 2-DVD set)
Watch the trailer at: **www.DyerMovie.com**

□ □

*am I being kind: how asking one simple question
can change your life,* by Michael J. Chase

BE HAPPY! Release the Power of Happiness in YOU,
by Robert Holden, Ph.D.

*THE EVEREST PRINCIPLE: How to Achieve the Summit
of Your Life,* by Stephen C. Brewer, M.D., and
Peggy Holt Wagner, M.S., L.P.C.

*EXCUSES BEGONE! How to Change Lifelong,
Self-Defeating Thinking Habits,* by Dr. Wayne W. Dyer

*THE OMG CHRONICLES: One Man's Quest to Discover What
God Means to People All Over the World,* by Peter Rodger

*PERSONAL DEVELOPMENT FOR SMART PEOPLE: The
Conscious Pursuit of Personal Growth,* by Steve Pavlina

*THIS IS THE MOMENT! How One Man's Yearlong Journey
Captured the Power of Extraordinary Gratitude,*
by Walter Green

All of the above are available at your local bookstore,
or may be ordered by visiting:

Hay House USA: **www.hayhouse.com**®
Hay House Australia: **www.hayhouse.com.au**
Hay House UK: **www.hayhouse.co.uk**
Hay House South Africa: **www.hayhouse.co.za**
Hay House India: **www.hayhouse.co.in**

ADVENTURE
IN Everything

How the Five Elements of Adventure
Create a Life of Authenticity,
Purpose, and Inspiration

Matthew Walker

HAY HOUSE, INC.
Carlsbad, California • New York City
London • Sydney • Johannesburg
Vancouver • Hong Kong • New Delhi

Published and distributed in the United States by: Hay House, Inc.: www .hayhouse.com • ***Published and distributed in Australia by:*** Hay House Australia Pty. Ltd.: www.hayhouse.com.au • ***Published and distributed in the United Kingdom by:*** Hay House UK, Ltd.: www.hayhouse.co.uk • ***Published and distributed in the Republic of South Africa by:*** Hay House SA (Pty), Ltd.: www.hayhouse.co.za • ***Distributed in Canada by:*** Raincoast: www.raincoast.com • ***Published in India by:*** Hay House Publishers India: www.hayhouse.co.in

Project editor: Patrick Gabrysiak • *Design:* Nick C. Welch

Library of Congress Cataloging-in-Publication Data

Walker, Matthew.
  Adventure in everything : how the five elements of adventure create a life of authenticity, purpose, and inspiration / Matthew Walker.
      p. cm.
  ISBN 978-1-4019-2960-2 (tradepbk. : alk. paper)   1. Self-actualization (Psychology) 2. Self-realization. 3. Quality of life. 4. Satisfaction. 5. Inspiration. I. Title.
  BF637.S4W346 2011
  158--dc22
                                        2010050119

ISBN: 978-1-4019-2960-2
Digital ISBN: 978-1-4019-2961-9

14 13 12 11   4 3 2 1
1st edition, September 2011

Printed in the United States of America

To Elizabeth, Elaine, and Zora.
For opening my life
to the full breadth of adventure.

CONTENTS

FOREWORD

Generally, the person who's invited to write a book's Foreword is responsible for endorsing its author, supporting its message, and suggesting that the reader consider a particular perspective as it relates to the work. I can do all three without hesitation and with great enthusiasm.

First, it's easy to endorse the book's author. I have known him for four years, and with each subsequent interaction, I continue to be impressed with his character and how much I learn from him. When our relationship began, I was Matthew's teacher, and he was my student. In short order, however, our roles reversed. Don't get me wrong. Matthew is a lifelong learner and brings a wealth of knowledge and experience to every conversation. However, I can't help but walk away from our interactions with a new perspective and a bigger vision of what is possible—not only for myself, but for the world in which we live.

Second, it's easy to support the substance of this book because it is rich and compelling, meaningful and insightful, honest and straightforward. Having explored and climbed the farthest reaches of the earth, Matthew brings his years of mountaineering experience to everyday life. He encourages you to think bigger about who you are, how you spend your time, and what you offer the world. With gripping stories of adventure and courage, he demonstrates the intrinsic value of appreciating every minute, stepping out of your routine, and embracing adventure in all aspects of your life: relationships, work, play, and more.

Third, as you read *Adventure in Everything,* I suggest you consider that thinking bigger about who you are and what you offer the world is not just a path toward personal and professional success, but also toward personal and professional alignment. You need never climb Mount Everest. (It's the last thing I'd be interested in doing.) But instead *define for yourself* what it means to think bigger about who you are and what you can offer. What does it mean to you to find more adventure in your everyday life?

As attractive as it may be to imagine that you can determine what the future will look like, it's just not possible. The future is uncertain. But if you embrace the philosophy that life is an adventure worth embracing, you will not simply focus on the number of days you have left or the quantity of activities you can pack into a day, but on the quality of each day you are lucky enough to live. If you do, you will find meaningful, fulfilling, and maybe even thrilling adventure in pursuing your dreams, expressing your values, and living your life.

Go for it. And remember to always think big (no, bigger than that)!

— **Michael Port**,
the *New York Times* best-selling author of four books,
including *The Think Big Manifesto*

□ □ □ □

PREFACE

What if every day when you woke up you couldn't wait to start your job? What if you spent your morning commute reflecting on all of the cool things you did the previous weekend, including trying out a new activity with your family or going on an incredible hike? What if your workday consisted of doing something you loved so much that you couldn't even believe someone wanted to pay you to do it, and when you got home, you had all the energy you needed to walk around the living room with your kids clinging to your legs and then to still be able to read them their favorite book for the 47th time when they were finally ready to go to sleep? What if you went to bed with your significant other while reflecting on all of the great things you were going to share throughout the rest of the week?

This all might sound like a 1950s commercial for tract housing, but believe it or not, there really are people who live this way. They enjoy working at their jobs, raising their families, and participating in whatever activities unfold as they move through their day-to-day lives. They pursue these various aspects of who they are with a sense of fulfillment, purpose, and satisfaction. If we were to construct a list of all the things these people have in common, some items that would be at the top might include a sense of contentment, an abundance of smiling, and even an ability to overcome whatever struggles they encounter.

They would also fill their lives with *adventure*. The goal of my company, Inner Passage, is to facilitate once-in-a-lifetime adventures to reconnect individuals with their leadership potential in their professional and personal lives. We are at our best when we are engaged in adventure, and I work with my clients to help them find this out for themselves through workshops, seminars, rock-climbing camps, and even mountaineering expeditions. When we maintain a spirit of adventure, we achieve outstanding and amazing things.

The purpose of this book is to teach you the significance of adventure and how pursuing some aspect of it in everything you do will help you attain the quality of life that has just been described. *Adventure in Everything* will provide you with a series of exercises and other tools that reflect the work I do with my clients, and which you will use to determine what's possible for you in a constructive and positive way.

The Introduction reveals the Five Elements of Adventure that are integral to fulfilling the mission of Inner Passage. What follows are five sections, one for each element, that will instruct you on how to apply them in your life. Finally, the Afterword will give you the necessary tools to take the first steps in finding your own version of purpose and satisfaction. You'll read stories about people who embody the message of this book, and I'll share many personal moments that have helped me develop these concepts.

When you wake up, go to bed, or do any number of things that fill up your day, do you feel the same sense of fulfillment as those who always rave about having had all of their dreams come true? If you do, then you've attained something that very few people ever have.

If you don't, then it's time to read on. The tools within these pages will help you find that life for yourself.

□ □ □ □

THE FIVE ELEMENTS
OF ADVENTURE

A lot can change at 800 feet off the ground. When someone is that high up, tall trees resemble shrubs and vehicles look like Matchbox cars. At that height, a few pieces of climbing equipment aren't just a random assortment of objects, but rather, the only things ensuring that the number 800 doesn't rapidly decrease to 700, 600, and straight on down to 0. At that height, the only thing still in focus is what lies ahead.

For me, on one day in the year 2000, that happened to be how high I was off the ground as I looked up at the toughest 150 feet of rock tower of a nearly 1,000-foot climb.

I had joined my mentor Geof to climb a summit in North Cascades National Park. (Geof is 30 years my senior, and we met in 1995 when he and I participated in a wilderness-medicine training outside of Seattle.) Since we didn't have the ability to anchor a rope at the peak of the tower, we were doing what's called *lead climbing.* Geof's decades of experience as a climber earned him the role of being the lead climber for this last 150 feet, which meant that he went ahead while placing protective fixtures into cracks in the rock. These points would lessen the distance that either of us could fall as we ascended the tower—so we could only fall as far as the length of rope that hung from the last protection placed. I'd racked up eight years of rock-climbing experience; worked as a mountain guide for several of those years; and led expeditions in Nepal, Argentina, Alaska, and many other places throughout the world, but as the last 150-foot pitch was the crux of the wall, I was grateful for his suggestion that he take the lead. He was preparing to do so when he turned to me.

"All set, Youth?"

I looked at my mentor. For almost the entire five years we'd known each other, we had an unspoken understanding that he always called me "Youth," but I never once would call him "Experience."

"Actually, Geof, I'm struggling."

"What are you talking about?" he asked as he started preparing the rope. "You're climbing strong. You're moving fast, with confidence and ease, and you're not even winded."

"I know, but—"

"It looks like you're in the best climbing shape of your life."

"It's not the climbing, Geof. I'm struggling with what to do next."

"Well, that's why I'm taking the lead on this last pitch, Youth. You just have to belay me." He gestured to the rope in my hand as he said this. I'd be managing the slack as he made his way to the summit, and then I would climb with the safety of the rope he'd expertly secured to the wall.

"No," I said. "It's Liz."

"Liz?" he echoed. "Is everything all right?"

"Well, yeah, but it's just that—"

"Just what?"

"I'm going to ask her to marry me."

Geof looked at me and then responded: "And you're struggling with whether or not she's going to—"

"Oh, no, no, no. I'm just thinking that I should take the full-time technical-writing job."

"Technical-writing job? Why would you do that?"

"It's the right thing to do, isn't it? Leading expeditions keeps me away from home at least five or six months out of the year. How could I be a good husband to her if I'm living fee to fee? How am I supposed to get good insurance? How can she rely on me if I'm always away?"

"Is that the lifestyle you lead now?"

"Well, no."

"And when you two met in '94, did you say to her that it was your dream to one day become a full-time technical writer so that you could get good insurance coverage?"

"Come on, Geof. I—"

"Did you?"

"No. Of course I didn't say that."

"Matt, Liz wants to share her life with you because of who you are—not who you should be or who the world expects you to be. Think about it: is it better to create your life on your terms, or someone else's?"

When I considered this, I not only couldn't ignore the fact that by being an international mountain guide I was doing exactly what I loved, but that in the last year or two I'd started to figure out that climbing wasn't just about not getting winded by the end of a pitch. My recent experiences on the job had taught me that there was an enormous mental struggle for both me and my clients that needed to be explored. What if there was something to be gained not just from continuing to do what I loved, but from challenging myself to see this new aspect through?

And would Liz even want to marry a man who didn't continue to find satisfaction in everything he did?

"I understand," I said.

"There's a different way of thinking, Youth. Here . . ."

I looked at the rack of climbing equipment he'd just handed me.

"Geof—"

"You're going to lead us to the summit. And here's your metaphor: just like you have to refocus your thinking to take over as lead climber, it's time for you to consider a new way of thinking about whether or not you want to find an Adventure in Everything you do."

The summer sun began to cast a long shadow across the wall in front of us. I looked at my shadow, now holding the equipment.

"Adventure in Everything," I repeated. "I like that idea."

The Five Elements of Adventure

As you're reading this, I'm sure it's quite obvious that I didn't take the technical-writing job. I chose to heed Geof's advice: I married Liz and continued to be an international mountain guide.

To further flesh out my understanding of how we may pursue our lives with a sense of adventure and fulfillment, I eventually scaled back this work to pursue my master's degree in behavioral science; and with it I began to formalize my investigation of how people make decisions and shape their communications in response to leaving their comfort zone in a conscious way. Instead of developing my skills through this more formal framework, conducting workshops across the country, and writing the book you currently hold in your hands, I could still be at that technical-writing job right now, enjoying my regular salary and the prospect of one day telling my daughter about all of the good sales-training manuals I'd written that day. Of course, there wouldn't have been anything wrong with these choices, had that ultimately been what I'd wanted, but even just a short conversation with Geof illustrated to me that this wasn't the case.

Even if most people haven't climbed a 1,000-foot rock tower with their mentor in the middle of the state of Washington, most can relate to the struggle that I expressed to Geof in relation to making a major decision about my life. Instead of choosing whether to take a desk job or to continue being a mountain guide, perhaps you had to figure out whether or not to pursue a new opportunity that would require you to move across the country, or you had to contend with leaving a secure corporate position to go into business for yourself. Maybe when you were younger you had to pick between attending the college your parents graduated from to study accounting or going to a conservatory to train as a clarinetist, or between starting a family or traveling the world.

Regardless of the specific decisions we make throughout our lives, at the heart of each one is the chance to examine ourselves; to make changes that increase our sense of possibility and accomplishment; and to have a life of authenticity, purpose, and inspiration. At the heart of each choice we make is the potential for adventure.

> *When you approach everything with the spirit of adventure, you infuse your life with vitality and radiance.*

In the Preface of this book, I asked you to consider whether or not you feel fulfilled. I suggested that finding Adventure in Everything you do can help you engage the world around you in a way that's deeply satisfying and joyous. This may sound like something reserved for the naturally spontaneous or particularly wealthy, but the simple truth is that everyone has this potential. How might you accomplish such a goal for yourself? What does it ultimately mean to find Adventure in Everything? Below is an introduction to the Five Elements of Adventure that I've developed over the last ten years.

1. Adventure Requires Us to Seek the Highest Endeavors for Ourselves

Had I taken the technical-writing job, I would have enjoyed a regular salary. I would have also enjoyed dependable health benefits, a general sense of stability in not always needing to find more work for myself, and a situation that never took me away from my soon-to-be wife. However, I wouldn't have been doing what I loved.

In 2000, I'd started to explore the physical challenges of leading climbing expeditions while also investigating the significant mental challenges that went hand in hand with my—and my clients'—experiences. Looking back on it, taking the safe, secure position would have been an inaccurate reflection of who I was. That decision would have stifled my potential for growth. Eventually, I experienced drastic progress in finding a way to successfully balance the professional demands of being a guide with the opportunity to start a life with Liz.

Element #1 of the Adventure in Everything framework is called *high endeavor*. To aim for a life with high endeavor is to set goals for ourselves that are worthy of our energy, love, and passion. But to pursue something of high endeavor, we must understand what is most important to us. When I decided not to accept the desk job, I understood that discovering the finer points of balancing my professional and personal lives was a goal of tremendous importance to me. (We'll explore more about high endeavor in Element #1.)

> *High endeavor is the combination*
> *of our dreams and passions.*

2. Adventure Requires Us to Embrace Uncertain Outcomes

When I decided to remain in my career as a mountain guide, there was no way for me to know how the future was going to turn out—or if it was going to turn out at all. I didn't know what sort of jobs I'd be getting a year from then, whether I was going to find a way to unravel the thoughts I'd begun to have about the mental and emotional challenges of climbing, or even what would happen next. This could be true of any situation, of course, but there would have been a much greater chance that I could predict the outcome of the next couple of years if I'd taken the writing position.

Element #2 is known as *uncertain outcome.* By its very nature, adventure suggests not knowing how something is going to turn out. I like to remind my students and clients that any endeavor with a predetermined outcome is *not* such an experience, but rather a "prepackaged" situation, much like an amusement-park ride. Relating an endeavor to the certainty—or, ideally, lack of certainty—of its outcome is a litmus test for adventure.

I knew that continuing my work as a mountain guide wasn't an adventure just because I was traveling to countries such as Kenya and Thailand—I'd already been to both places several times—but because I didn't have any way to predict how the trips would turn out. In this sense, they fell into this category because of the uncertainty of their outcomes.

> *Real life is a series of uncertain outcomes, and coming to peace with this concept allows for opportunity. Opportunity activates adventure.*

3. Adventure Requires Us to Totally Commit to a Chosen Endeavor

After Geof and I finished our climb, I returned home. I then proposed to Liz; went to graduate school; and taught the Five Elements of Adventure through many expeditions, workshops, and other educational venues. Deciding to go in this direction might have been a significant move, but that wasn't where the work ended. If I had chosen this path and then attached myself to preconceived ideas about what it would look like—as in focusing only on end results such as having an impressive résumé and earning a lot of money—then I'd have completely undermined the importance of having chosen this path in the first place.

To be *totally committed* to an endeavor is to pursue it with flexibility about its outcome, detachment from its results, and complete and total focus on the task at hand. Element #3 of the Adventure in Everything system, *having total commitment,* helps us place less importance on the *quantity* of our efforts, and instead emphasizes the *quality* of our efforts. Regardless of the challenges we encounter and the benefits we reap, having total commitment provides us with the ability to apply all of our skills toward success.

Had I not made a total commitment to becoming the best international mountain guide I could be, then the very reason for choosing this path—to create a satisfying life on my terms—would have become completely obsolete. (The section that covers this topic, Element #3, will teach you how to use this quality in all that you do.)

> *Total commitment is born from remaining centered, from letting go of the outcome.*

4. Adventure Requires Us to Tolerate Adverse Situations

After my fateful climb with Geof, I continued to be a mountain guide and never ran into a single obstacle. The end.

That's not exactly a convincing story, is it?

Not only is it unconvincing, it's not what happened. As I continued along the path that I chose, I encountered many challenges, including finding an appropriate balance between my professional and personal lives, struggling to determine what my clients were experiencing above and beyond the physical demands of climbing, and retraining myself to function in a classroom after being a number of years removed from a college environment. Each time I came upon adverse circumstances, it seemed possible that I wasn't going to succeed.

Adventure demands a high *tolerance for adversity.* Element #4 teaches us to be nimble in the face of seeming defeat. When we encounter a difficult situation while attempting to accomplish our goals, we can either succumb to defeat or turn the situation into an opportunity to find more creative—and therefore more fulfilling—ways to triumph.

When we pursue our endeavors with a tolerance for adversity, we're able to conduct ourselves with style, grace, humility, and humor. When I faced situations such as being away from home for long periods of time while in a committed relationship, I created a solution that allowed me to have adventure *and* accommodate space for a relationship simultaneously. (The section on Element #4 will demonstrate how to pursue what we desire while embracing the challenges that likely lie ahead.)

> *Tolerance for adversity is the single biggest predictor of success.*

5. Adventure Requires Great Companionship

It's no accident that my revelatory climb in North Cascades National Park happened in Geof's company. Aside from the fact that climbing that wall would have been terribly dangerous—if not outright impossible—without a partner, having the guidance and company of a friend and mentor helped me use the experience as a way to work through a particularly significant decision. Had he not been there as a sounding board and a source of feedback, I could have very well made a different, less desirable decision.

The events that have the greatest impact and leave the most indelible marks all share one common ingredient: *great companionship.* When I look back on all of the adventures in my life, I find that Element #5 is the single most important one. When we pursue our endeavors with the benefit of the company of others, we have the opportunity to give unselfishly, receive sincere feedback, support one another, and work together to reach goals that are unattainable on our own.

To have great companionship is to share a sense of trust; and because I was able to trust Geof to be honest with me, and trust my wife to accept me for who I am, I was able to identify my highest purpose in life *and* pursue it. (The section on this fifth and final element will

provide an outline of how to identify great companions
and how to *be* one as well.)

> *Sharing adventure with great companions*
> *is the icing on the cake.*

*High endeavor, uncertain outcome, total commitment,
tolerance for adversity,* and *great companionship* are not
lofty aspirations intended for a select few; they are the
makings of an inspiring and approachable framework
for anyone seeking meaning and rejuvenation in his or
her life, work, and personal relationships. What follows
are several concepts and practical tools that will help
you to successfully learn this framework and apply it in
a meaningful way.

The Beginner's Mind

I'd like you to stop reading at the end of the next
paragraph. Upon putting the book down, think about the
last time you were upset about not receiving a phone call
from someone who was supposed to get in touch with
you. If it was a call expected from a colleague, remember
the frustration you felt because your ability to do your job

was based on this person. If it was a call from a potential romantic partner, recall the hurt you felt as you realized that he or she wasn't as excited about the relationship as you were. If it was a call from a friend or family member, reconnect with your resentment as you assumed that this person was neglecting the relationship.

Now close your eyes and breathe for 15 seconds. Rather than dwell on any of those missed connections, simply focus on nothing but your breath. Notice that you're inhaling when you're inhaling, and exhaling when you're exhaling. If, after only five seconds, your mind starts wandering and you begin thinking of things unrelated to your breath, then try again. When you've managed to sustain concentration on your breath for the entire 15 seconds, pick up the book again and resume reading.

□ □

Welcome back. If you followed the instructions and were able to direct your attention solely to your breathing and nothing else, you took the very first step in finding Adventure in Everything you do. You were able to focus completely and entirely on the task at hand, rather than on the actions of other people and the world beyond.

The most important part of finding Adventure in Everything is to conduct ourselves with humility, grace, and a willingness to be who we are. Rather than live in this way, however, most of us allow our contentment to be based on the individuals and circumstances around us—for example, we don't experience satisfaction until we find out that our romantic partner didn't call because his or her cell phone died. We are only able to accept ourselves when we're accepted by others, as opposed to feeling comfortable in our own skin.

By focusing on our breath, we can recognize that our thoughts are not our reality. Instead of concentrating on those things outside of ourselves that are beyond our control, we're able to slow down and be less impulsive or reactive. Breathing helps us let go of whatever stories we've created based on our own insecurities, and ground ourselves in our own reality. Each time we're confronted by a situation beyond our control, we can come back to the breath. When we do so, we're one step closer to following our dreams.

Now, imagine what would happen if a friend gave you a birthday gift in the form of an opportunity to participate in an oil-painting workshop over the course of a weekend—even though you have absolutely no experience creating visual art. Along with the gift, you get a brochure that describes the workshop as a beginner's course. Despite the claim that you don't need to have any prior knowledge of the activity, and despite your affection for the friend who gave you this gift, you aren't at all excited about going. In fact, you're absolutely terrified. As soon as you picture yourself in a studio applying paint to canvas, you start thinking about how you've never been able to draw stick figures, everyone else at the workshop is likely to be better than you, and the teacher will probably tell you that you're so bad you're no longer welcome. This isn't such a difficult scenario to imagine, because that's usually what happens when you're presented with an opportunity to leave your comfort zone, right?

Often, if not most of the time, we respond to uncomfortable situations by telling ourselves why they won't work out well: *I can't take a painting workshop because I don't even know how to draw stick figures. I can't start a family because I don't know if I'll still have a job a year from now. I can't pursue my dream career because that's something that only happens to sophisticated city people and the wealthy.* Invariably, we spin ourselves a tale that starts with "I can't," is supported with "because," and is based on a fear that we're not good enough. It's understandable that we're afraid of what might—or might not—happen if we set out to pursue our dream career, for if we set a goal that's really that important, then there's the potential that the results won't meet our expectations.

When you made a conscious effort to focus on your breath in the previous exercise, you may have created a story as to why you shouldn't. You might have thought that it was weird, wanted to keep reading, or simply felt that holding your attention on your breath for 15 seconds was too hard. By succeeding, however, you were able to put aside your excuses, concentrate completely and entirely on the task at hand, and let go of any latent angst stemming from a missed connection over the phone—as well as any preconceptions about what should or shouldn't be happening beyond whatever was necessary to accomplish that task. This exercise was your introduction to the *beginner's mind*.

The beginner's mind is a concept that comes from Buddhist teachings. It's the choice to engage in an endeavor, thought, or emotion with the express desire of embracing all possibilities. When you undertake an activity with the beginner's mind, you consciously withhold judgment of yourself and others. You refrain from telling yourself a story that may distract or deter you from the purity of the experience, and instead focus entirely and completely on the task at hand. If, in the above scenario where you're given the brochure for the workshop, you said to yourself, *Wow, I've never really painted before—it will be interesting to see what this experience is like,* then you've accepted all possible outcomes. Upon arriving at the class, if the instructor told you to try a painting exercise and all you did was follow his or her directions, you've practiced having a beginner's mind.

> *To live with the beginner's mind is to see*
> *the world through the eyes of a child.*
> *In this world, anything is possible.*

Steve's Adventure

Just as many people have, Steve attended one of my mountain-climbing expeditions in Arizona. But one thing regarding his participation that was of particular significance was the fact that he'd never been rock climbing before. In fact, he'd never even camped out in the woods!

However, Steve was intrigued with the Adventure in Everything program. He wanted to see how it could support him as he embraced a new vocation and set a new vision for the rest of his life. Attending his first-ever climb was certainly going to afford him this opportunity.

In his mid-50s at the time of this adventure, Steve had a successful career leading private and public companies. He had lived in many different cities throughout the United States, had traveled the world, and had two sons who were already starting families of their own. His oldest son loved the outdoors, and even though he'd never been rock climbing either, Steve invited him to go along as a 30th-birthday present.

When considering this climb, Steve expressed concern to me about his lack of experience. Over the course of several conversations, I assured him that in my role as guide I could ensure his safety during the three days we'd work together. When the necessary precautions are taken, I told him, mountain climbing is safer than driving a car from Phoenix to Tucson.

At the opening campfire, when we discussed each climber's motivation for taking part in the program, Steve's son noted that, although he'd been given this wonderful opportunity as a birthday present, he could sense that his dad just really needed him to be there. Neither of them realized that their already strong and open relationship would deepen as a result of climbing together, while expanding their individual understanding of what was possible.

The first day, we all took part in a technical orientation that taught the fundamentals of climbing, and then by the second day, we were on our way up the mountain. Steve kept up with everyone else and followed directions well; in fact, he and his son were a successful team. About midday, as Steve was climbing, he lost his footing on the mountain and fell about three or four feet, which covered the amount of slack available in his rope. With a slight hesitation, he resumed his climb but fell again only seconds later. Neither his son nor anyone else could see him anymore, for he was now dangling out of sight in a crevice in the wall. His son simply said, "You've got this, Dad. Just remember to breathe."

At the evening campfire later on, Steve's son recalled how his father had then let out the deepest grunt he'd ever heard and within seconds emerged and continued his ascent. Steve reported that in that moment—when he let out that grunt—he was the most determined he'd ever been in his life, which was evident as he climbed with more grace, focus, and confidence than he had the entire day and a half we'd been working together.

He had let go of all judgment and had allowed himself to live closer to his edge.

□ □

This story bears on the concept of the beginner's mind for several reasons. Having never been climbing before, Steve could have very easily decided not to participate in this expedition because of a tale that started with "I can't" and continued with "because," such as "I can't go climbing because I've never had any experience doing it and wouldn't know what to do." Instead, he did everything that was asked of him, arrived at camp physically prepared, and had all the required clothing and equipment.

Steve's willingness to be vulnerable—a key element of the beginner's mind—started with him looking to his son for companionship and support. He then engaged in the activity without any expectations. When it was time to learn the mechanics of tying knots, he tied knots. When it was time to learn how to belay his partner, he did so.

What was more significant, though, was Steve's experience after his fall. When he recounted what had happened, he reported that in the moment he fell the second time, he realized that the one fear that was holding him back—the fear of falling—was also keeping him from completely and totally immersing himself in the present moment. Before he slipped, he'd created a number of stories such as "I can't get my foot up to that hold because I might fall if I miss," "Falling is failing," "Others will think I'm weak if I fall," and "I have to look good for my son." When he actually did fall, though, he allowed himself to let go of all these stories and simply relax into the present moment.

For the rest of the weekend, Steve let go of any presumptions about climbing and released his fear. He was a quintessential example of someone who utilized the beginner's mind.

Throw Away the Old Story

My main purpose in sharing Steve's story is to illustrate how the beginner's mind can be applied to any situation and will benefit the pursuit of any goal. When we release our expectations about a positive outcome, or a perceived lack of ability to ensure that outcome, we're able to focus all our attention on the steps we're taking along the way.

If you think back to the breathing exercise, you might agree that employing the beginner's mind is not an easy thing to. It's much easier to tell a story of why you *can't* do something instead of just doing it. It would be quite simple to put this book down right now, create an excuse for why you can't create what you've always wanted, and continue living as you always have.

One way in which you can help yourself decrease the likelihood that you'll follow old, fearful behaviors is to simply get rid of them. To throw away your old story, write a letter to yourself that identifies what has blocked you from doing what you really want. Maybe you've always intended to go back to school to become a filmmaker but felt the time for that has passed. Or do you want to lose weight but have never found the discipline to make this happen? This letter is intended to help you let go of whatever you've told yourself, in favor of thinking with the beginner's mind. I highly suggest that you write it on a separate piece of paper and in the structure that follows:

Paragraph #1: Identify what you want. Using one of the above examples, this paragraph might begin: "I want to go to school to study filmmaking." Then explain why this is important to you.

Paragraph #2: Describe the reasons you've always given yourself as to why you haven't pursued this endeavor. You might begin: "I've never gone back to school because I've always had this idea that film school is filled with 22-year-olds who attend keg parties on the weekends." Now list all of the justifications you've given yourself as to why you can't go after this dream.

Paragraph #3: State what not aspiring to this goal has cost you. This paragraph might begin: "Every time I go to work, I'm left with a feeling that there might be a more satisfying life for me out there." Be as dramatic as you can in illustrating this sense of loss.

Then sign the letter. Once you're done, you can read it out loud, read it silently to yourself, or just fold it up and put it in an envelope. The most important thing at this point, though, is to get rid it. Tear it up. Put it through the shredder. Burn it.

Knowing that you put as much effort as you could into composing the letter and were as honest and articulate as possible in telling this story, let it go. By destroying it, you're freeing yourself of all the reasons not to pursue what you desire. Once you've released what has never served you, you're ready to find Adventure in Everything with the help of the beginner's mind. Before continuing to the next section, put down this book and write that letter *now*.

The Journal

Have you ever had one of those days in which you had too many thoughts running through your head? Did you then completely escape from it all, perhaps by reading a tabloid magazine or zoning out in front of the TV? It's likely that you have, for this has become a standard formula for modern living. We completely overwhelm our lives with a thousand different tasks and worries, and then try to "self-medicate" with the most basic forms of escape. We create challenges for ourselves, but rather than work past them, we let them pile up and then hide them when they become too overwhelming.

In contrast to perpetuating this lifestyle, the intention of this book is to teach you how to not only hold yourself accountable for your actions and choices, but to help you instigate positive change. Those who seek Adventure in Everything believe in the possibility that they can ultimately get what they want in life—they just have to take responsibility for making it happen.

If living with the beginner's mind is a way to embrace the concept of finding adventure, then keeping a journal is a way to more tangibly commit to this process. Throughout these pages, I'll be instructing you to actively journal about the progress you're making as you learn and apply the Five Elements of Adventure to your life. This is to be a living document, a sacred place where you can organize your thoughts or get them out of your head. It can be as simple as a notebook you buy at the local store, or something a little fancier that costs a bit more. One thing it must have, however, is blank pages. Before finishing this chapter—in fact, even before finishing this section—go out and buy your journal. Pick up this book again once you've made this purchase and are ready to begin using it.

> *One of the key components of change is account-ability. Having a journal will keep you from making excuses for growth not taking place.*

As you've now bought your journal, you've made a personal, tangible commitment to explore the Five Elements of Adventure. There are two basic ways in which you'll use this journal, and I've outlined each of them in the following sections.

Organized Writing

Throughout the book, I'll be offering you different concepts to consider as a way to begin utilizing each of the five elements. One of the best methods to apply these teachings in a practical style is to create charts, lists, and other passages that will help illustrate certain aspect of your life. You'll be asked to evaluate the nature of your endeavors and identify their outcomes. In completing these activities, you'll be able to use your journal as a tool to assess your situation and goals with objectivity. By committing to writing with focus, you'll be better prepared to examine your life with authority and confidence.

Stream-of-Consciousness Writing

Just as writing in a detailed and organized manner can help you address your personal situation with authority, stream-of-consciousness writing can help you purge yourself of whatever thoughts may be cluttering your mind. This technique is the act of putting onto paper whatever comes up in your mind exactly as it emerges. It can be rambling, grammatically incorrect, incoherent, and generally lacking the structure outlined in the previous paragraph. The point of this activity is not to win a Pulitzer Prize, but instead to use the pages of your journal as a "brain dump."

Earlier in the Introduction, I commented that many of us suffer from being completely overwhelmed by what is in our own heads. Well, practicing stream-of-consciousness writing gives us an opportunity to release all of this in a concrete way.

One of the most important components of this activity, however, is resisting the urge to go back and read the content. The goal is to help you purge these overwhelming thoughts, not to pass judgment on something you needed to let go of during a challenging period. When you write in this way, you're giving yourself the opportunity to free your mind without the burden of judgment.

Throughout these pages, I'll suggest moments that will be valuable opportunities to employ this technique, but it's my hope that this activity will become a habit you'll continue to use beyond this book.

Your First Journal Exercise

To break in your journal, I'd like you to try 15 minutes of stream-of-consciousness writing. Jot down whatever arises in your mind about what you want from your life. It's of tremendous importance that you use the whole time rather than stopping to think for five minutes about what you should write next. For instance, you might start off by writing something precise and coherent such as "I want to attend film school . . ." but then wind up with "I really have no idea what to write. I'm not sure what the point of this is. I need to remember to buy eggs on my way home from picking up the kids. Somewhere along the way I'm going to have to end this sentence with a period." The goal of this exercise is to simply put whatever comes up in your head on the page. Give yourself permission to write without judgment. Grab your journal and a pen, and set a timer for 15 minutes.

Once you've finished, instead of going back and reading what you wrote, observe how you feel after having gotten all that "stuff" out. Consider whether or not you feel lighter and if you have fewer thoughts running around in your head.

□ □

Now that you've been introduced to the Five Elements of Adventure, have started your education on the beginner's mind, and have broken in your journal, you're ready to begin exploring the elements in greater detail. Much as I did when I set out to find my way as a mountain guide and a family man all those years ago, you're on your way to creating something bigger and better for your life.

Now is the time for you to find your adventure.

Introduction Task List

At the end of the next five parts of the book, each of which examines a different element in-depth, you'll find a task list that recaps the activities I'll be asking you to complete. What follows are those from the Introduction:

- Think about the last time you were upset about something or someone. Rather than dwell on the problem, spend 15 seconds breathing, focusing on nothing but your breath.

- Write a letter to yourself that identifies what has gotten in the way of doing what you really want in life, and then destroy the letter.

- Purchase a journal that you'll be writing in as you make your way through this book.

- Try 15 minutes of stream-of-consciousness writing in your new journal. Then take the time to consider how you feel after having completed this exercise.

HIGH ENDEAVOR

If you open the back of the book *Curious? Discover the Missing Ingredient to a Fulfilling Life,* you'll see that its author, Todd Kashdan, Ph.D., is a clinical psychologist and associate professor of psychology at George Mason University. You'll learn that along with conducting research related to curiosity, happiness, and other aspects of life, he's received awards for his work and has been featured in a variety of media outlets, including *The Washington Post* and NPR.

What you might have to dig a little deeper to find out, though, is that Todd wasn't always on this track to becoming a published author and celebrated psychologist. Before he found himself in this field, he worked on Wall Street. Not only that, he was very successful at what he did.

Although he was quite good at his job in the financial industry and lived comfortably, Todd realized only a few years into his career that he wasn't even slightly fulfilled by what he was doing. Rather than continue on the path he was on, he took some time to figure out that finance wasn't what he wanted to do, because he didn't feel that it had any sort of constructive impact on others. Sure, this profession allowed him to make lots of money, but to what end? Eventually, Todd realized that he needed to do something with his life that allowed him to analyze people and provide helpful feedback to those in need of making positive change. His career as a psychologist and author was the result.

□ □

Nici Holt Cline was pretty content with life. She had earned a degree in art, enjoyed cooking for friends and family, and wrote a blog that chronicled her exploits in the garden. She then went on to get a job as an advocate for the arts at a local museum in Montana . . . and fell in love with it. She planned to expand her advocacy career by going to grad school in Chicago for two years—while being away from her husband for all that time—so that she could one day direct a not-for-profit organization of her own. Mother Nature seemed to have her own path in mind, however, for not long before Nici was to start school, she got pregnant.

Several things then happened after this development:

- She shaped her blog to focus on the more personal aspects of being a mom.
- She left her job at the museum once she gave birth to her second child.
- She increased the readership of her blog each week.
- She began to use her background in art to design children's clothes.

She did not, however, wind up going to grad school.

Just about anyone who reads the content of Nici's blog, **digthischickmt.com**, will soon discover that not only did she completely embrace her role as a mother, she also set higher standards for herself. Regardless of what she'd originally planned to do in arts advocacy, she accepted the opportunities she was given, and with them the possibility of seeing greater beauty in all aspects of her life.

What Is High Endeavor?

What would have happened if Todd had chosen to never leave the finance industry or Nici had refused to fully recognize her role as a mother? Well, Todd would have moved along in his career—earning a comfortable salary—while always having a sense of longing for something that was more fulfilling and true to who he was. Nici would still be a mother, but rather than look at her situation as an opportunity to experience joy, she would see everything she did for her family as yet another task that took her away from the job she wanted and felt she should have been doing. Of course, in both of these examples, Todd and Nici *didn't* choose this far less appealing path for themselves. Instead, they decided to embrace the first element of finding Adventure in Everything: high endeavor.

In the Introduction, I explained how high endeavor is a goal that's worthy of our energy, love, and passion. We set plenty of goals for ourselves in any given day, month, or year; and most of them typically fall into a category of *low* endeavors. For example, we bemoan our need to take out the garbage, drag ourselves to the post office to mail the rent check, and fulfill another annual sales quota for a company we've worked at for more than 15 years.

At any given moment, we can be moving toward accomplishing a dozen different long- and short-term goals, yet it's common that none of them are worthy of our interest—let alone our love or passion. At best, the most that many of us can wish for is to move through the tedium of our day and then spend the evening fantasizing about a more exciting world we don't expect to ever know.

To better illustrate this idea, I like to ask my clients to imagine a rubber band that connects two poles. The first pole represents the current reality of daily tasks, such as taking out the garbage and fulfilling quotas, and the second represents the future they're committed to. For most people, this second pole tends to still symbolize the garbage and quotas, since the only future they're able to see for themselves is a continuation of what they're doing now. In that sense, it's located just in front of the first pole, and the rubber band is barely stretched, if it's even taut enough not to fall right to the ground.

However, when we decide to pursue a high endeavor in response to a life that hasn't previously stirred our love and passion, we're inciting a fundamental paradigm shift in how we live. Essentially, we're moving the second pole farther from the first one, and in doing so we're stretching out the rubber band to cause what's called *creative tension.*

Perhaps you leave the finance industry to study positive psychology and become a teacher and author, quit your job at a museum and create a blog and clothing line out of your adoration for your role as a parent, or do something else entirely. Regardless of *what* you do, call upon this creative tension to imagine a more fulfilling, purposeful, and satisfying life for yourself. Create a high endeavor.

> *"The significant problems we face cannot be solved at the same level of thinking we were at when we created them."*
>
> — ALBERT EINSTEIN

High Endeavor and Fear

Now, go find a life of fulfillment and purpose.

Wait, you can't just find fulfillment and purpose because someone told you to? Is something standing in your way? According to a 2010 *Seattle Times* article by Jeannine Aversa entitled "Americans' Job Satisfaction Falls to Record Low," it seems that "only 45 percent of Americans are satisfied with their work." If all it took for people to find purpose in their lives was to hear someone *tell* them to do so, then we could just give each other this advice on the street or in the elevator, and that percentage would go way up. As a result, our satisfaction with all other aspects of our lives would increase as well.

Of course, it's usually not this simple. Every time we set out to do something different—be it finding a new job, taking up a hobby, or asking someone out—one type of emotion usually creeps in: *fear.* We become afraid of what other people will say behind our backs if we leave our cushy job at a law firm to write articles about fishing, fret about whether or not we're really going to stay in shape by practicing yoga, or imagine a hundred different scenarios that could occur if we ask out that person from the coffee shop . . . and these scenarios ultimately lead to our humiliation and utter failure.

We may not even feel burdened by our own fear of a new path, but we might be concerned about everything that's projected onto us by others. Friends, family members, and anyone else we know might tell us outright that we can't create change for ourselves. They might even resent us for setting out to do what they've never been able to do for themselves.

This is why it just isn't enough for someone to come up to you on the street and tell you to find a life of fulfillment and purpose. Often there are too many fears, what-if scenarios, or other problems that attempt to convince you that finding adventure isn't possible—that high endeavors are only set by wealthy, elite, athletic people who go on mountain-climbing expeditions in Nepal. Your life must instead be filled with garbage you don't want to take out, rent you don't want to pay, and quotas you don't want to fulfill.

Quite frankly, this isn't the case. The basis of the system outlined in this book is that each one of us really can find Adventure in Everything. We all have the potential to imagine a different future for ourselves and go after it with all of the passion and determination that those wealthy, athletic individuals seem to have.

This pursuit will cause a fundamental shift in your life; and in teaching you about high endeavor, I'm inviting you to give yourself permission to find this shift.

When it comes to discovering Adventure in Everything, fear is of very little use. Later on you'll have the opportunity to work toward overcoming it in a constructive way.

> *If the future isn't big enough, it collapses into current reality.*

Imagine a High Endeavor for Yourself

Again, it might feel fine to give yourself permission to find high endeavor, but that doesn't necessarily mean that doing so is easy. It's not as if there's a simple way to envision something that encapsulates all of your interests, passions, and dreams into a single lifestyle.

Or is there?

The truth is that there really *is* a method for imagining your high endeavor, and it's actually quite simple. In fact, it's embarrassingly easy. The formula is as follows:

activity you enjoy + activity you enjoy + activity you enjoy = high endeavor

In other words, seeking a high endeavor simply requires you to take several of your interests and combine them in some way. For example, let's say that three of your greatest passions are cycling, travel, and philanthropy. If you were to apply this formula to your life, then a high endeavor for you to pursue would be to go on a trip to Hawaii and participate in some sort of cycling event that raises money for a cause you believe in. Perhaps you've traveled the world, participated in countless fund-raisers, and been cycling almost every day for the past ten years, but the pursuit only turns into a high endeavor when the activities you're enthusiastic about become intertwined in one basic experience. If all three of these things really were of interest to you, do you think that going on that trip would invoke a sense of passion? I imagine that the answer is an inarguable *yes!*

This formula can, of course, be applied to all aspects of your life, including what you do for a living and at home. In Todd's pursuit of a career change, he combined his interest in psychology with his love of writing and teaching to form what essentially amounted to the ideal job. In Nici's case, she combined her love of sewing, art, photography, and her family to write a popular blog and become a clothing designer. If a high endeavor is worthy of your love and effort, then combining your interests to focus on one undertaking ignites your passion. It really is that simple.

Take a moment right now to write down three activities that you enjoy in your journal. Then brainstorm ways they could be joined together into a single high endeavor.

What If You Draw a Blank?

It might be fine for people who already know they love philanthropy, travel, and cycling to plan that great trip to Hawaii, but what if the interests to be plugged into that formula aren't so obvious? What if you, like so many people, only know that you're not satisfied with your current situation; but when asked what kind of situation you'd prefer, you draw a blank?

Typically, when you're asked a question that you don't know the answer to, you'll use a more systematic way of thinking to solve the problem. You'll make your determination by saying something to the effect of "If *a* and *b*, then *c*." For example, if you know that you want to go out to dinner but don't know what type of food you want to eat, you might conclude, "If I had Chinese last week, and Italian the week before that, then it's time for me to have Mexican." If you don't like your current position as an office manager and want to find another job, you might say, "I'm stuck in an office all day and feel like I'm in prison, so I'm going to become a park ranger so I can work outdoors."

Mexican food may be exactly the sort of meal you have a taste for, and perhaps you really would enjoy being a park ranger; however, assigning value to either of these solutions based entirely on this logical, analytical process can be profoundly limiting. You may find that you really do love Chinese food and want to have it a second week in a row, or there could be another type of cuisine out there that you'd enjoy more than any of these other options.

Further, you may feel imprisoned by your job, but it doesn't necessarily have to be because you're in an office. Maybe your particular workplace is an oppressive and stifling environment. It's also possible that you really are ideally suited for this type of position, but you just need to find a more inspirational company. The main point here is that regardless of the specific choices you make about what you decide to pursue, making them entirely with your left brain can severely limit your potential for creating experiences for yourself that you can feel passionate about.

What's the alternative to thinking this way? The left brain is what we use to solve problems analytically, while the right side relates to imagination and creativity. People who predominantly rely on the latter are often those with professions such as artist, composer, or novelist. Utilization of the right brain, though, isn't limited to individuals with these careers; and it's certainly not just for painting, composing music, or writing books.

Everyone uses this imaginative, creative side; and it also helps solve all sorts of problems. For instance, you decide against the Italian restaurant when you suddenly remember that riverside café that a friend raved about a few months ago. Or you realize that if you take a couple of classes in computer systems and databases, you'll greatly increase the number of companies that you could be hired by. Ultimately, when you draw a blank while thinking about a high endeavor—and about solving pretty much every other problem in life—you can use your imagination to find an answer.

Now, if we tell anyone older than seven to use his or her imagination, it's likely that we'll be greeted with raised eyebrows or some other expression of cynicism. Surely that sort of "woo-woo" stuff isn't for those who live in the real world and have to take care of things like grocery lists and property taxes, right? The sad truth is that using our right brains isn't any more child- or hippielike than using the left brain, but somewhere along the line someone decided that this was the case. Whether it's because our imagination didn't help us when the mean kids picked on us at recess, or our school district cut the arts budget by the time we got to high school, most of us learned pretty early on that if *a* and *b* happen, then *c* must be the inevitable result.

Find a Place of Inspirational Beauty

An extension of finding a shift in your life is to explore this more imaginative aspect of yourself. To do so, I'd like you to take your journal to a place of inspirational beauty and practice stream-of-consciousness writing. A place of inspirational beauty is any location that fosters a sense of reflection and calm.

You may think that I'm talking about a bench in the quiet corner of your local park or a grassy area along the stream in your backyard. However, it could also be somewhere that isn't necessarily an obvious place of reflection. Perhaps you love supporting your local minor-league baseball team, sitting up in the nosebleed section and reflecting on your life while the fans around you are yelling and screaming. Maybe you grew up several towns away but almost never visit your old haunts, and going back to have a slice of pizza at the local joint reminds you of a simpler, less stressful time in your life. Regardless of where your place of inspirational beauty might be—and despite what someone else might think of it—go there with your journal and take a seat.

Now, with the sound of water trickling, the smell of hot dogs wafting, or the taste of garlic still on your tongue, put pen to paper and start writing about whatever it is that you want right now. Do this for 15 minutes; then stop to become aware of your surroundings once again. Then start writing for another 15 minutes. Follow the instructions on stream-of-consciousness writing found in the Introduction, be sure to put anything that's in your head on the page, and don't go back and read it. The point is only to conduct a brain dump and release all of the logical, analytical thoughts you have. Once you've freed your mind, you're left with an imagination that will, quite possibly, reveal an answer for what sort of endeavor you might be passionate about.

Of course, there are no guarantees that this will happen right away. It could take ten trips to the baseball stadium and then moving into the college hockey season before a single idea emerges. No matter how long such a process takes, you'll be doing yourself a significant service by freeing your mind of unnecessary thoughts.

Still, without an inkling of what new endeavors to pursue—or even if you know what you'd like to do but don't think it's feasible—you could easily get discouraged from creating more adventure in your life. The next section will explain what can be done under these circumstances.

Begin with the Possible

It can become quite discouraging to want to create more adventure in your life but not have an idea of how to get started or feel that such opportunities aren't possible. Twenty hours of stream-of-consciousness writing may yield no inspiring ideas, and a cycling tour in Hawaii might sound fantastic but be completely unfeasible without the money and vacation time to make it happen. This is why it's important to remember that you don't have to go on a mountain-climbing expedition in Nepal to find Adventure in Everything you do, and that bringing something to fruition can begin with what's immediately possible.

Nici had the intention to go to school and study a subject she loved, and many might think that giving up such a possibility in order to raise children would be a step down into a more mundane existence. There are, after all, billions of mothers throughout the world. Clearly, though, she embraced her role as a parent and found creative, expressive ways to explore it through her blog and clothing line. If we're unable to think of endeavors that reflect our passions, or we feel that we lack the time and money to do what we want, we can follow Nici's example of using our current situation as a platform for inciting passion in more nuanced ways.

Perhaps you're working as an office manager but would love nothing more than to go back to school to become a pastry chef. Or maybe you simply find your job to be drudge work that takes you away from your family. With your parental responsibilities and a mortgage to pay, however, you don't feel that anything but this particular reality is possible.

What you could do, though, is spend Sunday afternoon preparing baked goods to share with your co-workers the next day in the office. You could even enlist the help of your children so that you're doing something together as a family. By providing delicious treats to very grateful people each week, you'd also be creating a more positive work environment, taking advantage of an opportunity to pursue your interest in baking, and bridging the gap between work and family in a way that's immediately possible.

If you find that your greatest passions aren't really accessible to you, then take your journal to your place of inspirational beauty and write in a stream-of-consciousness fashion about the various ways in which you could merge your interests with your current situation. You might find that not only are you able to successfully combine your interests and obligations, but other things start to happen as well: someone at work who knows a food distributor could fall in love with your baking, and suddenly you have a whole new enterprise to explore!

Perceived Risk vs. Actual Risk

Earlier we explored the significance of fear. To begin putting your fears into perspective, I'd like you to do a perceived risk/actual risk exercise in your journal. People often find themselves reluctant to make changes in their lives because they decide that such a change "isn't worth the risk," as might be the case with someone who wants to be a pastry chef but has responsibilities at home. In your journal, draw a line down the middle of a page. At the top on the left side, write the words "Perceived Risk."

On the right side, write the words "Actual Risk." In the "Perceived Risk" column, begin writing down endeavors you've always wanted to pursue but never took the time to learn more about using the following format:

I can't [insert endeavor] *because* [insert uninformed assumptions].

Then, in the "Actual Risk" column, write down the real reasons why you aren't able to take action right at this moment if there are specific tasks standing in your way:

I don't think I can [insert endeavor] *right now because I've never* [insert the information necessary to be more informed].

An example of this exercise for the person who has always wanted to go to school to become a pastry chef is:

Perceived Risk: *I can't <u>become a pastry chef</u> because <u>I'm too old, the school is too expensive, and it will take me away from my children.</u>*

Actual Risk: *I don't think I can <u>begin school right now</u> because I've never <u>researched school possibilities, learned more about financial aid, or cultivated a proper support group for helping me with my children.</u>*

The point of this is to help you focus on learning more about your endeavor instead of assuming that it isn't possible. You might not be able to start school right away, but you can definitely find out more about the possible places to study, take a weekend trip to visit one or two of them, and learn about affordable student-loan options. In reflecting on your high endeavor through the Perceived Risk/Actual Risk exercise, you can give yourself a more informed idea of what's actually possible.

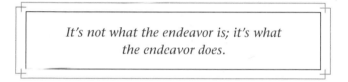

It's not what the endeavor is; it's what the endeavor does.

Confirm the Compatibility of Your Endeavor and You

Have you ever watched a biopic about somebody famous, or even read a biography of someone in an influential field, and marveled at how committed the person was to pursuing his or her goals . . . or lamented how this individual's life turned into a sad, empty echo of what he or she once aspired to be? In response to watching one of these films or reading one of these books, did you start to wonder how a biography of *you* might be told, and even start to compare the progress of your life with that of the main character?

Although you might feel silly for doing so, thinking about your own life as a biography can be more than a flight of fancy. It can also be a significant tool in determining the nature of an endeavor you're aspiring to.

When you search for a high endeavor as the basis for finding Adventure in Everything, you run into the possibility of pursuing an activity that isn't compatible with what you actually want. You may know that your current situation isn't right for you, but then look for something else in response that, while different, isn't true to who you are as a person. You might hate your job but seek out a career path that makes you feel just as empty and unfulfilled. Perhaps you think that you weigh too much and want to feel healthier and fit, but your solution is to lift weights and run on a treadmill even if you hate doing both of these activities.

Even though it's good to be aware that your current life isn't what you want, it's very important that what you choose to do instead is compatible with your interests and values. The way to establish whether or not your new endeavor is compatible with you—therefore truly making it a *high* endeavor—is by looking at your life as an autobiography.

Write an Autobiography

At the end of this section, I'd like you to put this book down again. When you do so, open your journal and write a short autobiography that goes up to the present moment. In a sense, this will be as if you're writing your own obituary, since you're going to need to keep it concise and to the point. This exercise is not, however, intended to be morbid or scary.

This autobiography should only be two paragraphs long. In the first paragraph, describe the general aspects of your life, including highlights of your educational background, the various jobs and careers you've had, who's in your immediate family, how you spent time with your closest friends, and what you liked to do for fun and recreation. In the second paragraph, explain *how* you lived—as in what you enjoyed the most about your life, what you liked the least, how others close to you might describe you, and how you would characterize yourself. Keep the entire autobiography under 500 words. Go ahead and write it now.

Values

Next, I'd like you to study the following list of values. A *value* is a quality or attribute that you may aspire to embody in any activity or task that you participate in. For instance, when you make plans to become a parent because you seek out the satisfaction and fulfillment of having a family, you most likely aspire to create *generosity* throughout your interactions with your family members and *stability* in your home.

But if you didn't intend to become a parent and felt obligated to marry the person with whom you conceived a child, you'd possibly regard the same responsibility in a negative light. Instead of generosity, you might aspire to the value of *indebtedness*—in that you might look at every minute taken up by your familial responsibilities as currency that they must in turn pay back to you. Further, instead of stability, you might seek out *rigidity,* where you must maintain order and discipline in the home or else the life you feel that you've already lost control of will only become more chaotic.

This is, of course, an extreme reaction to becoming a parent, but the example is intended to demonstrate how any one value in life can have two sides of the same basic experience: if you don't regard your commitment to your family as an opportunity to give, then you expect payment for services rendered; and rather than seeking the warmth and tenderness that comes with a stable home, you enforce your dogma.

These two views aren't intended to be construed as right and wrong, for if strict observation of rules and discipline is wrong, then following the law would be wrong as well. Instead, they reflect positive and negative intentions, or higher and lower endeavors. Being generous with others and pursuing stability is likely to afford you greater opportunities to experience passion and fulfillment than expecting indebtedness and enforcing rigidity.

Given this, the following list of values is intended to demonstrate the distinction between the qualities of high endeavors (the first italicized word) and low endeavors (the second italicized word). It will also be helpful in completing the exercise that follows.

- Making a *commitment* to follow through on a task and experience satisfaction, or having an *attachment* to the results of the task and setting yourself up for disappointment

- Seeking *abundance* in which you can live a fuller life, or seeking the *accumulation* of wealth so that you can have more material possessions

- Exhibiting *generosity* by giving to others, or expecting *indebtedness* in exchange for your actions and deeds

- Working toward *stability* in your home and livelihood, or enforcing *rigidity* in the behaviors and actions of those around you

- Seeking *enjoyment* in the experiences you have, or exploiting all aspects of living to the point of *indulgence*

- Maintaining your *health* for the sake of feeling good, or aspiring to *perfection* for the sake of vanity

- Desiring a *leadership* role in order to facilitate positive experiences, or exercising *manipulation* over others for the sake of having your way

- Allowing yourself to have a good sense of *humor* for the sake of increasing everyone's enjoyment, or subjecting others to *ridicule* for the sake of overcoming your own insecurities

- Participating in *expression* for the sake of creating honest emotional reactions in others, or contributing *censure* for the sake of putting down what you don't understand

- Offering *performance* for the sake of providing entertainment to others, or indulging in *narcissism* for the sake of building yourself up on other people's time

- Maintaining *focus* on a project with the intention of sharing it with others, or having an *obsession* with the project at the expense of fulfilling your responsibilities

For each pair of values, there's either a positive or negative intention. Those who strive for positive values are much more likely to find the interest, love, and passion that will ultimately lead to having more purpose.

Write an Autobiography . . . Again

The final step in determining your compatibility with the endeavors you'd like to pursue is to write one more autobiography. This time, however, instead of discussing your life up until this moment, create one that covers your whole life as if you'd lived to be 80 or 90 years old. Although it will make brief mention of the events leading up to this point (education, jobs, family, and so on), I want you to put a much greater emphasis on what you wish for yourself from the present moment on. If you're floating around without any professional focus, this autobiography can describe the career that you'll eventually find. If you're single and interested in meeting someone to settle down and start a family with, this is your opportunity to describe the nature of that path.

Somewhat similar to the style you used before, the first paragraph should describe what you hope to have done, and the second paragraph will explain how you wish to have lived. This is where you have total permission to reach as high as you want to live the embodiment of all your dreams and passions. If you've always wanted to be a skydiving instructor, then here's your chance to illustrate how that happened. If your ambition is to live in one of those gorgeous houses on the other side of town, then here's where you reveal what you did to make it so.

The catch, though, is that not only must you describe your ideal life, but you must use at least five of the positive values outlined in the previous bulleted list. For example, let's say that you had a standard office job; were a single mother to three children; and, while you only did seasonal work for a florist on the side, you knew that helping people plan their weddings was the perfect combination of your interests and passions. An example of a sentence that you might have written in the first autobiography exercise is: "I worked as a manager at the local insurance company and sometimes moonlighted at the local florist during wedding season." Now, in regard to the career you hope to create for yourself, you might say: "When I turned 38, I began to create more *abundance* in my life when I opened my own business as a wedding coordinator; as a result, I was better able to provide *stability* for the home I shared with my three children."

The purpose of including these positive values in this second autobiography is that it will require you to step up and put your greatest desires on the page. Saying that you hit the lottery and accumulated all sorts of wealth at age 38 might seem like a nice idea, but since it doesn't reflect a positive intention to create abundance, it's likely to be something that you aren't honestly passionate about. Like the first story, keep this one under 500 words.

The main point of this exercise is to provide a framework for how to make the best choices. You may be considering a new endeavor that could be labeled as high, but if it doesn't fit into this new life, then it's not likely to provide much fulfillment. Therefore, it isn't compatible with who you are. Before reading on, write this second autobiography and then refer back to the endeavors you've imagined for yourself. If you find that they fit into this new vision, then it's time to move on to the next step. If not, simply put the book down and reflect for a couple of days, or visit your place of inspirational beauty and unload your thoughts once again.

> *Seeking positive values fosters higher endeavors, and pursuing higher endeavors leads to Adventure in Everything.*

Engage Others in Regard to Your Endeavor

The next step in pursuing a high endeavor is quite simple. As soon as you've imagined it for yourself and confirmed that it's compatible with who you are, you must engage at least one person in a dialogue about it. The purpose of this is to help you find out more about the goal to ensure that it's going to serve you in the way you intend and that you'll experience greater success in your pursuit. If you set out to get a master's degree in English literature with the ambition of one day becoming a college professor, you might soon find that this is a fiercely competitive field in which it's almost impossible to get a job without a Ph.D.

Instead of jumping right in, it's important to ask someone with more knowledge in your area of interest about its ins and outs. If you want to become an English professor, talk to one of your own college professors about this goal. If you'd like to learn how to decorate cakes, ask the local pastry chef about his or her job or go online and find a community of people who do this as a hobby or career. If your desire is to start a family, ask friends who have already done so about the implications of such a decision. Engaging people in this way will both serve to help you gather more information and lay the groundwork for great companionship (which is the fifth and final element in the Adventure in Everything system).

> *Receiving help in reframing our own assumptions and beliefs can adjust our structure of interpretation. We can then create a future from this new and different place.*

Write a Letter of Commitment to Yourself

How often have you bought a self-help book that provides a template for how to change your life, but once you read it, you put it down and simply picked up another one?

For most of us, what usually happens is that we like the ideas presented, but when it comes to actually committing our time and energy to making the changes that the author has recommended, we blow them off. This not only stalls the possibility of a real shift taking place, but it's a waste of time.

It's my intention that this book be about more than simply indulging in a nice idea for a few hours. For this reason, I've instructed you to stop reading and do an exercise at several points, and I'd like you to do so now. Draft a letter of commitment to yourself that will charge you with the task of pursuing the high endeavors you've laid out while reading about this first element of Adventure in Everything.

This letter should be very simple. Please write it as if it's for somebody else—for example, you'd say "You have lived for 35 years" instead of "I have lived for 35 years." It should consist of three paragraphs.

The **first** paragraph explains how the life you've led up until now hasn't served you in the best possible way. You may even want to use a few of those negative values that you outlined earlier.

The **second** paragraph outlines what endeavors you'd like to pursue. Be sure to make statements such as "You will earn your Ph.D. and become a professor" or "You will start your business as a wedding coordinator."

The **third** paragraph describes the first steps you must take to make your endeavors a reality. Be sure to use language that's direct and precise: "You will go to graduate school part-time for the next four semesters" or "You will volunteer to coordinate your sister's wedding next spring."

At the end of the letter, make a basic statement about how important this is for you, such as "Pursuing this endeavor will help you attain passion, love, and fulfillment, so it's important to follow through and make this happen." Sign your name at the bottom, place it in an envelope, and affix the envelope to the inside back cover of this book with a paper clip or any other type of fastener that you have available. Whenever you feel distracted from accomplishing your goals, take out the letter and read it for inspiration to stay on track.

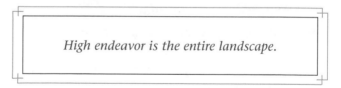

High endeavor is the entire landscape.

Whether you're setting out to start a whole new career like Todd, taking your new role as a parent to the highest level like Nici, or doing something else entirely, the foundation of finding Adventure in Everything is creating high endeavors for yourself. Before moving on to the next sections of this book, be sure to use the exercises I've provided to gain a precise idea of how you're going to make changes for yourself in the weeks and months to come.

High-Endeavor Task List

- Think about three activities you enjoy and find a way to combine them into one basic endeavor. This is an example of a high endeavor you could pursue for yourself.

- Take your journal to a place of inspirational beauty and write in a stream-of-consciousness fashion regarding what your high endeavor might be.

- Practice the Perceived Risks/Actual Risks exercise to help reframe your mind-set with respect to how you can become more informed about your endeavor.

- Draft your autobiography up to this point in your life in two paragraphs, keeping it under 500 words.

- From the perspective of your 80- or 90-
  year-old self, write a second autobiography
  that incorporates at least five of the positive
  values described in this chapter.

- Compose a letter of commitment to
  yourself.

UNCERTAIN OUTCOME

The line is long. It stretches out past the pavilion, where it's guided by the metal barriers that allow people to snake back and forth past each other every few minutes. The first sign you pass not only says that you must be 48 inches tall to get on this ride, but also that the wait from this point is 60 minutes. The next sign says that the wait is now 45 minutes, even though it's been at least 30 since you passed the last one. As you enter the pavilion, you catch a glimpse of the first hill a good 100 yards away, and you can even see a car making the ascent, only to plummet back down toward the earth.

You start to wonder what the hell you were thinking when you decided to get in line for this roller coaster.

Eighty-five minutes after you entered the 60-minute line, you make your way to the area where the next round of passengers position themselves to enter the cars they'll be riding. As you and your neighbor are about to take your spots in the space reserved for the second car—the line for the first is far too long—you're cut off by a man and his son, who claim the space for themselves.

"Excuse me, sir," you say. "I believe we're supposed to be next."

"No, you are *not* next," the man hisses as he moves his son behind him in response to the obviously menacing threat your polite tone suggested. *"Pay attention."*

You look around for an attendant to intervene, but realize that this misunderstanding was born of the fact that this ride—and this theme park as a whole—is severely understaffed. You then look to your riding companion, who shrugs with a blank look on his face, and resign yourself to the fact that the few minutes you'll be delayed waiting for the next ride isn't worth the amount of conflict you'll create if you pursue this any further.

Eventually, it's your turn. You enter the car, and the safety harness locks into place as you guide it over your head and shoulders. You then look to your neighbor with that eager, childlike smile reserved only for the most highly anticipated moments in life. The car jolts as it advances out of the pavilion, and you roll out into the sun.

Just like that, you're off. Unlike those rides that use a chain system to get you over the first hill, this one starts you off in a shock of speed. One second you're still, and the next you're traveling at what the brochures and television commercials say is 128 miles per hour. You begin to ascend that first hill you saw an hour ago, and, like the cars you also saw, you only barely make it over the top. You're sure you left your screams back at the peak, for the descent is so fast and so . . . *vertical* that you might as well be breaking the sound barrier. Improbably, there's a flash of light as you enter a loop, and you wonder if you were simply seeing things as you go right into a double corkscrew, another loop, and the second steep drop before the car makes a sharp turn and then finishes off with the standard series of camelback hills that has ended nearly every roller-coaster ride you've ever been on.

After disembarking, you waddle down the exit ramp and try to reorient yourself to the ground. As you begin to relive the experience you just had, you notice a series of screens. One of them displays your picture, taken right after the longest descent—perhaps you really did see a flash after all. You don't remember screaming quite as much as the photo suggests, but the ride happened so quickly that you barely remembered any one moment in particular.

You already knew it was going to be short, however. You were told the ride was one minute and ten seconds long, and it lasted for exactly that amount of time.

Life Is Not an Amusement-Park Ride

Consider for a moment some of the choices you've made that have had a significant impact on you. For example, what schools did you attend? Who have you decided to spend your life with? What was the first career you pursued? Where was the first place you moved after you left your childhood home? When did you have kids? When did you write a book or start your own business?

Next, consider how different your life would be if each of those choices had been gift wrapped with a guaranteed outcome. What if you knew what job you were going to have before you even started your freshman year of college? What if you decided to have a boy and a girl born three years apart, and that's exactly what you got?

On the surface, these situations sound pretty good, don't they? In each one, you have complete control. You are free to carefully craft, mold, and develop your path with the absolute assurance of the best possible result. Regardless of whether or not this sounds good, it does seem just a bit ridiculous, doesn't it?

However, this is precisely what we often attempt to do in our lives. We try our hardest to guarantee an outcome for every situation, and we go out of our way to maintain control of all the different variables. For instance, we predict exactly where we see ourselves in 5 years, even 20. This is not only a maddening proposition, but it's a losing one. It's as if we're wrestling a ghost.

Now, think about the roller coaster featured in the previous narrative. What happened during that initial shock of speed? It provided a thrilling rush of adrenaline, and then perhaps a moment of terror when it felt like the car wasn't going to make it over the enormous hill. The experience was entertaining and momentarily exciting, and for $14.95 it could be captured forever in a souvenir photo. It was, nevertheless, only a ride. It led you on a predetermined path to those thrills, without causing harm to you or anyone else who's at least 48 inches tall.

But by the time it delivered you safely back to the loading platform, what were you left with except for a self-contained and predetermined experience? Aside from the long line and the conflict with the man and his son, you went on the ride without incident and continued with your life. In truth, a roller coaster, for all the fun it might provide, is just a temporary reprieve from the uncontrollable realities of the real world. It will always last for one minute and ten seconds—no more, no less.

We all need a certain allotment of prearranged outcomes in our lives . . . a little control. We also benefit from having routines, such as being sure to always brush our teeth before going to bed, and arriving for work on time every day. To neglect consistency would not only be irresponsible, but it would likely lead to chaos. However, habitual activities and predetermined consequences can only serve as backdrops for our growth as human beings. They aren't vehicles for inspiration or illumination, and certainly not for finding Adventure in Everything. As explained in Element #1, adventure is born from our pursuit of a high endeavor, and the litmus test for determining the potential for that is through Element #2 of this system: *uncertain outcome.*

Uncertain outcome is exactly what it sounds like: an end result that's unknown at the outset of a pursuit. An amusement-park ride, for all its thrills and excitement, may be immediately gratifying to the senses, but it is in no way beneficial to you in the long term. An endeavor with an uncertain outcome, then, is filled with rewarding possibilities. For example, taking a new job, starting a family, or opening a business is one that you have the potential to grow from. The final tool for determining whether or not your goal truly is a high endeavor is to determine if you know what its result will be.

If you know what's going to happen, then it isn't a high endeavor. Instead, it's simply another activity that fills up part of your day.

> *Uncertain outcome is the test that determines*
> *if your high endeavor is <u>truly</u> a high endeavor—*
> *or if it's merely an amusement-park ride*
> *with a predetermined outcome.*

Seek Uncertainty in Your Life

Why should it even be necessary to explore the topic of uncertain outcomes as its own element in the Adventure in Everything system? Shouldn't it be enough to simply say that we need to find endeavors in which we don't know what the result will be and leave it at that?

Of course, while the concept of uncertain outcomes is simple, it's not always easy to put ourselves in situations that exemplify this quality. Not knowing how something will turn out opens us up to the possibility of not succeeding, of feeling like a failure, or generally brings about a sense of pain or loss if things don't go the way we want them to—it ultimately causes us to feel fear.

It may be immediately gratifying to grab a burger and fries at the local diner, but we all know that eating a meal of vegetables, whole grains, and lean proteins will provide greater benefits in the long run. The same is true for seeking uncertain outcomes in our lives: it may be scary, and it might not be as pleasing in the short term as something else that has a more certain outcome, but it will provide us with much more of an opportunity for growth and fulfillment over the course of our lives.

The goal of the remainder of this section is to not only teach you the significance of uncertain outcomes while you're pursuing adventure, but to present you with an outline for how to accept more uncertainty. And this happens through three basic steps:

1. *Recognizing* that it's lacking in your life

2. *Accepting* that it's perfectly human to experience trepidation in response to the unknown

3. *Embracing* uncertainty as a staple of your life

> *The struggle for control is unwinnable. It's you fighting you for control of the uncontrollable.*

Recognizing Uncertainty

It is now time for you to spend a few minutes taking what I call an "Adventure in Everything Personal Inventory."

Grab a pen; flip to a blank page in your journal; and make a list of all the projects, endeavors, tasks, and activities that fill up your day. This can be an inventory of the routine aspects of your life, such as playing a sport once a week at the local recreation center or knitting each evening before you go to bed, but it should also include your ongoing relationships, vocation, major projects, hobbies, commitments, and whatever else you're currently pursuing. In a stream-of-consciousness fashion, begin listing *everything* you're involved in. Keep in mind that it doesn't matter if you do so in calendar order, or how many items you might have. Just keep writing.

Once you feel your inventory is complete—or at least well under way—go back through each item and label it as an endeavor with a certain or uncertain outcome. For example, if you're working at a job that has a predetermined schedule, a steady salary, and a precise set of responsibilities, it has a certain outcome. If you're in a career where you make your own hours, your income can change from month to month, and the job description shifts as you find new and different projects, then it has an uncertain outcome. If you have a hobby that calls upon you to repeat the same activities each week—such as knitting—then it has a certain outcome. A side project that could potentially turn into a new career, such as writing a book or making and selling jewelry, has an uncertain outcome.

Here are two hypothetical inventories for you to consider and model your own list off of. Take a look:

Inventory #1

Getting married	Uncertain outcome
Becoming a father	Uncertain outcome
Working as an accountant	Certain outcome
Volunteering at a soup kitchen	Certain outcome
Cooking	Certain outcome . . . usually
Taking a class in painting with watercolors	Certain outcome

Hiking	Certain outcome
Playing in a weekly card game	Certain outcome
Golf	Certain outcome
Going to the movies	Certain outcome
Playing in a softball league	Certain outcome

Inventory #2

Getting married	Uncertain outcome
Owning a business	Uncertain outcome
Writing a novel	Uncertain outcome
Becoming a Big Sister to a disadvantaged youth	Certain outcome

Going on a rock-climbing expedition	Uncertain outcome
Playing in a weekly tennis game	Certain outcome
Taking part in a book club	Certain outcome

In Inventory #1—which was clearly written by a man—his roles as a father and husband are the things on the list that have been designated as uncertain outcomes. You probably noticed, though, that he has a long list of other endeavors that are certain in their outcomes: he knows that he's going to get 18 holes of golf in the next time he visits the course, and at the end of his time in the kitchen, he will have cooked a meal . . . usually.

In many ways, this might seem like a fabulous existence, for what man wouldn't want to be able to balance his work life with sports, card games, classes, and even the good feelings associated with volunteering? However, while the list of activities may seem diverse and appealing, if he continues living in this way, every aspect of his life—with the exception of his experiences as a husband and a father—will be exactly the same in 30 years as it is now. In the meantime, he will have very little adventure; he will rarely endeavor to seek more fulfillment than he does currently, and he's likely to look back wishing he'd tried mountain climbing, started his own business, or authored the book he always wanted to write. It's likely he will have wanted more for himself . . . only by then it will be too late.

In the case of Inventory #2, which was written by a woman, there are decidedly fewer endeavors on the list. However, what do you notice about them? Even though this person has also gotten married, nearly every other endeavor on her list has an equally uncertain outcome. In fact, she's pursuing many goals that the man might wish he could incorporate into his own life, such as writing a novel and owning a business. While the woman might not ever sell her novel, find success through her business, or make it to the top of the mountain, she'll most likely look back with fewer regrets. She's defining her life on her own terms, and although she's pursuing fewer endeavors than the man is, they'll ultimately lead her to feel more empowered and fulfilled, and likely cause her to play a much more positive role in the lives of others. If all she ever did was play tennis and participate in a book club, she might have an enjoyable time, but she probably wouldn't feel any of the other qualities inherent in experiencing Adventure in Everything.

As I mentioned, the first step in embracing uncertainty is to recognize that your life *lacks* this quality and is generally defined by routine and predetermined outcomes. Therefore, your task is simple: after creating your personal inventory, assess whether or not your current endeavors favor certain or uncertain outcomes. If you're a spouse and a parent, but otherwise fill your days with endeavors that have set end results, then recognize that to find Adventure in Everything you must pursue activities—hopefully those you conceived for yourself with the help of Element #1—that will inspire greater uncertainty and therefore create greater potential for fulfillment.

Recognize that the world is complex. The number of variables affecting any given endeavor is astounding; and while you play a part in the outcome, you have influence, but not full control, over your circumstances. If your inventory reflects the one created by the woman in Inventory #2, and you're already pursuing many activities with uncertain outcomes, then that's fantastic. You're already incorporating uncertainty in your life, and the following elements in this book will help you strengthen your commitment to whatever it is that you're pursuing.

> *The adventures in life are rich with moments of uncertainty and, in part, are defined by this uncertainty.*

Accepting Uncertainty

Has the following ever happened to you while checking out at the grocery store? There are three different registers open, and the first one has three customers already waiting in line, each with a dozen or so items. The next register has only two customers in line, but they both have well over 50 items in their carts. The third register, located all the way over by the store manager's booth, only has an elderly woman at it. But, you reason, she looks as though she will pay for her entire purchase in change and slow the cashier down by asking him too many distracting, meandering questions.

You choose to get in the first line, deciding that the three smaller checkouts will take less time than the other two lines, but then spend the entire time craning your neck to see if you would have done better to make a different choice. As it turns out, the cashier in the second line is tremendously efficient and gets her two customers out the door before your cashier even starts on the shopper in front of you. And then you notice a bagger come to help the third cashier, so the elderly woman pays and then proceeds to chat up the store manager in his booth for several minutes . . . before your first item even gets scanned. Had you made a different choice, you would have been out the door *five whole minutes* earlier; therefore, you spend the rest of your time in the store peeved due to all the moments you wasted with your horrible decision-making abilities.

We can all relate to having made some bad line-waiting decisions over the course of our lives. Not only that, but most of us quickly become frustrated as we stew over how time is ticking away.

Similarly, most of us can imagine experiencing anxiety and fear when we decide to pursue an endeavor with an uncertain outcome: we might fret over not knowing where our next paycheck is coming from, whether or not we're going to be a good parent, or what's going to happen if we venture to an unfamiliar country on a trip or expedition. The next step toward embracing uncertain outcomes in our lives is as simple as recognizing the need for uncertainty in the first place: *acceptance.*

You may not know where your next paycheck is coming from, if you're going to be a good parent, or if your trip will take you to places that force you entirely out of your comfort zone. However, you have two choices once you've created your own method of income, determined that you want to become a parent, planned an expedition, or picked a checkout line: (1) live with the anxiety, fear, or frustration; or (2) accept that some aspects of your future are out of your control. Instead of wasting your time fighting for control that will never be yours, allow yourself to be open to whatever happens, and know that you'll make do with what you have whenever it comes to you.

When you do find acceptance, you open yourself up to an entirely new way of living with the unknown. You might not know from what source your income is coming in, but without a set salary dictated by an employer, you have no limit to how much your bank account can grow. You may not know if you're going to be a good parent, but you have the possibility of creating a warm, nurturing environment for another human being who can prosper with your support. When you explore new places and locations, you collect stories and memories that you'll have for the rest of your life. Acceptance is a gift that frees up the energy you wasted trying to control the outcome, which then allows you to be present to potentiality.

Write a Letter of Caring to Yourself

Of course, finding the presence of mind to accept uncertain outcomes is easier to think and read about than it is to actually achieve. Going from being the person who gets frustrated over melting ice cream to one who accepts the question marks of being an entrepreneur will take time. Next we'll explore a couple of tools that can be helpful for embracing uncertainty in your life, but right now I'd like you to turn to a blank page in your journal and write yourself another letter.

Being accepting of uncertainty requires us to let ourselves know that yes, it has always been our tendency to be fearful of losing control, and yes, letting go of things we can't control is difficult . . . but we don't have to live like that anymore.

To get started on the path of welcoming uncertainty in your life, write yourself a letter in which you let yourself off the hook for putting too much energy into fear and anxiety of the unknown, reminding yourself that there is another way to live. Make this letter three paragraphs long.

In the **first** paragraph, describe how you typically relate to situations with unknown outcomes. Do you get anxious and lose sleep due to stress? Do you tend to indulge in vices such as eating unhealthy foods, drinking alcohol, smoking, or even just watching a lot of silly television? Do you become difficult when dealing with others, expressing irritability or frustration toward those who upset you? Write as if you're reporting these behaviors as objectively as possible—how they'd be described in a newspaper article. It may begin with language such as: "Up until now, you tend to get frustrated and angry when you've lost control . . ."

The **second** paragraph is where you'll send yourself a message of caring. In other words, you'll tell yourself it's okay that you've behaved in this way up until this point, and that you'll continue to do so many more times in the future. Remind yourself that this doesn't make you a bad person, nor does it mean you have less potential for adventure and fulfillment—it simply means that you're human. Feel free to borrow the language I've used in this paragraph as much as you'd like, or find your own way of letting yourself know that everything is going to be okay. What's most important, though, is that you treat yourself with the level of kindness with which you wish to be treated by others.

In the **third** paragraph, write a statement of intention addressing how you'll try to let go of the need for complete control. By doing so, you'll come to understand that uncertainty will provide the potential for greater possibilities. This paragraph may start with language such as: "It's now time to embrace uncertainty as an indication of a greater and more fulfilling life. You have the ability to do this, and as long as you continue to be kind to yourself, you have the potential to let go of anxiety and fear." Before reading on, write this letter to yourself and dog-ear its place in your journal so that you can reference it when you're struggling with a fear of the unknown.

> *When we decide to engage in uncertain pursuits, we discover a zest and enthusiasm that drives us to new heights.*

Embracing Uncertainty

Becoming a mountain guide was a relatively easy decision to make. I knew that it would give me the opportunity to be with others, travel to distant parts of the world, and experience new cultures. I also knew that I wanted to climb, but didn't have the money to fund my own trips. After talking with some people in the industry, I opened myself up to new opportunities and jumped at the chance to become an assistant guide on an expedition in Chile when a friend of a friend needed some help. Although there were some risks, such as having to quit my job in order to make this happen, I benefited from having good mentors, and made this decision from a grounded place.

As I alluded to in the Introduction, though, I wasn't without my own share of struggles in figuring out my professional career. I've already mentioned how I was unsure of my ability to be a good husband if I was always leading climbing trips, but soon after going to Chile, I had to make another difficult decision. I had to establish whether or not it would be worth it for me to go to grad school and take my work to a new level. I'd determined that my clients' experiences with mountain climbing weren't limited to overcoming the physical obstacle of reaching the summit, but these activities were also about opening people up to a new way of relating to challenges in all aspects of their lives.

Soon after I got married, I went back to school to study behavioral science. My hypothesis was that mountain-climbing expeditions weren't simply a matter of scaling rock walls, but rather microcosms of a more fundamental human experience: what happens when we open ourselves up to adventure. What if there was a way for each of us to relate to the act of seeking adventure even if there wasn't a mountain anywhere in sight?

While I was interested in discovering answers to this question, I couldn't just drop everything to pursue this further. I had responsibilities; I needed to consider my obligation to my wife; and, quite frankly, there was a strong possibility that if I did find a way to effectively communicate the importance of adventure, my proposition might not ever be taken seriously.

Given that you're now reading this book, you can see that I did decide to go to grad school, and, through this course of study, found a way to systematize the significance of adventure in people's lives. Ultimately, I ended up deriving greater satisfaction from the work I do, even though I had no idea if it would turn out this way. I was able to do all of this because I embraced an uncertain outcome.

□ □

There are many situations we've had in our lives that are defined by a seeming sense of loss or disappointment: we get laid off from our job, we come to the end of a relationship, or we don't get a gig that we've auditioned or applied for. While these experiences can be difficult and even painful to go through, there's a considerable flip side to each of them. Getting laid off from our job could lead to a better one, or even a new, more satisfying career path. Although we may feel hurt after breaking up with a boy- or girlfriend, this may cause us to find someone with whom we share a much greater chemistry. And being turned down for a position could leave us feeling rejected, but there may be two or three others that we hear about tomorrow with far greater potential.

Each of these circumstances catapults us into the unknown, but when uncertainty has been recognized and accepted, it can then be embraced as an opportunity for more desirable things to come. I might have felt fear over the possibility of developing a system that wouldn't be taken seriously or useful to others, but in following through, I considered it to be a chance at a more fulfilling career. In all of these examples, embracing uncertainty allows us to look at the future as a gift.

While doing so is an action to be taken, coming up with a high endeavor to pursue is not the result of accomplishing specific tasks, such as using stream-of-consciousness writing. The act of accepting the unknown is more a progression of the mind, and achieving this shift is the result of training ourselves to look at unforeseeable outcomes as circumstances for substantial improvements in life. In other words, and as I've just alluded to, no longer is having a job simply an *opportunity* to find another one that's more suited to our goals.

Given this more nuanced quality, I'd like to present you with an exercise that initiates what will ultimately be a long-term shift in how to relate to the unknown. You're better prepared to embrace uncertainty if you're more grounded in your current situation, and by feeling this way you can identify the first step toward pursuing your high endeavor with the "I can . . . if I . . ." exercise you did in Element #1.

Set up two columns in a page of your journal, much like you did with the Perceived Risks/Actual Risks exercise. At the top of the left-hand column, write the words "I can . . ." At the top of the right-hand column, write the words ". . . if I . . ." Next, list tasks in the left-hand column that are related to your high endeavor—no matter how small they seem. Then jot down individual steps you can take to accomplish each task. Using the example of being a pastry chef, you may use the two columns to write: *"I can raise money for culinary school if I get a part-time job and apply for a student loan."* Identifying this first step can make the larger picture of your high endeavor more immediately manageable, which will bring about a greater sense of being grounded in your pursuit. With stability, you can calmly take the first step into the unknown.

Recall how I encouraged you to engage others when collecting information about your high endeavors. Well, it's also helpful to seek support from those whom you trust and who you feel are sympathetic to the fact that you're learning to embrace uncertain outcomes. These are the people whom you can call up and get inspiration from when you have one of those oh-my-god-what-am-I-about-to-do types of days.

In contrast, there are probably individuals in your life who have a compulsive need to tell you why your goals won't work out, or even that they won't materialize at all. These are not the people to talk to in times of vulnerability and insecurity. Your goal is to work toward embracing uncertainty, and you don't need negative influences who reinforce your fears rather than help you recast them into something more constructive. (Element #5 will help you learn more about the significance of connecting with others.)

> *When we view our challenges as possibilities and opportunities, we are supported by two types of confidence: our own self-confidence and the confidence bestowed upon us by our community. Both are equally valuable.*

In the next chapter, you'll explore how embracing uncertainty can be fostered through a complete and total commitment to your endeavors. In this sense, you'll develop ways to practice being present to the challenges that often surface when the outcomes of your pursuits are unknown. Life is not an amusement-park ride, but is instead colored with uncertainty. In accepting this, you give yourself the gift of adventure that will forever enhance your appreciation of all you have and all you want to achieve.

Uncertain-Outcome Task List

- Use stream-of-consciousness writing to take the Adventure in Everything Personal Inventory.

- Determine if each endeavor in your inventory has a certain or uncertain outcome.

- Write a letter of caring in which you let yourself off the hook for putting so much energy into fear and anxiety about the unknown, while reminding yourself that there's another way to live.

- Practice the "I can . . . if I . . ." exercise to help ground yourself in your endeavor and embrace more uncertainty in your life.

TOTAL COMMITMENT

Molly Wizenberg was never really a goal setter growing up. Goals frightened her. Rather than set them and then feel pressure to accomplish them, she did what she felt like doing. She initially flourished in school, earning undergraduate degrees in biology and French and pursuing a Ph.D. in cultural anthropology. However, when she reflected on the aspirations—or *goals*—of her fellow students, including their desire to get research grants, receive tenured positions as professors, and publish on a consistent basis, she didn't quite fit this mold anymore.

Nevertheless, Molly traveled to France to study the country's social-security system for her dissertation. But rather than focus on all things related to the federalization of social insurance, she found herself captivated by the various food experiences available to her in this new and different world. She was unable to get enough of the breads, the cheeses, the wines . . . everything. She stared into bakery windows, ate at restaurants, and did everything she could to immerse herself in local gastronomy. When she wrote home, it was about wine. When she went to bed, she reflected on her evening meal.

In Paris, Molly realized that her first love was food. It was a staple of her childhood experience, and she'd felt a hint of embarrassment in response to her father's bragging about how much better their family meals were than what could be found at restaurants. As she grew older, though, she not only realized how great the food was, but how much the sharing of meals was a primary reason for the solidarity of her life at home. Whether she was studying French or anthropology, she found her affection for all things related to food at the forefront of her thoughts.

A lot happened in the five weeks following Molly's time in France. She broke up with her boyfriend; decided to leave graduate school; and paid tribute to her father (who had recently passed), scattering his ashes with her mother.

She also started a blog about food.

Molly had wanted to be a writer when she was a kid, but she'd quickly forgotten about that aspiration as she got older. When she was explaining to a friend how she'd decided to cut her Ph.D. program down to a master's degree because of what she'd preferred to spend her time doing in Paris, he suggested that she start a blog about food.

This struck her as an interesting idea. With a blog, she could reflect on her love of food as much as she wanted, and maintaining it would require her to write even when she didn't feel she had anything to say. Upon leaving grad school, she no longer had a precise professional track for herself. When confronted by this lack of structure, though, she didn't succumb to fears, but instead asked herself what would be the worst thing that could possibly happen. All she could come up with was that she might not have a job for a while or the satisfaction of a professional career.

On the flip side, however, Molly only had the potential for a net *gain* in happiness, for she knew that her current track wasn't providing any gratification at all. She promptly got a part-time job at a nonprofit publishing house and began writing a blog called Orangette (**orangette.blogspot.com**) in 2004. On this new path, she knew that for at least a part of her day she'd be able to focus on two things she was fascinated with: food and writing.

Within a few months of starting the blog, something remarkable happened. She started attracting readers other than her friends and family and established a presence in the new world of food blogging.

In early 2006, Molly got a book deal with Simon & Schuster to write *A Homemade Life: Stories and Recipes from My Kitchen Table*. She's likely to be very appreciative of your patronage if and when you buy this memoir. You'll enjoy reading about how she embraced what made her feel most like herself—writing about food— just like the thousands who have already bought the book and helped it become a *New York Times* bestseller. She also contributes a column to *Bon Appétit* magazine on a monthly basis.

There was a time when Molly Wizenberg struggled to figure out what she wanted do for a living. Because she was able to let go of any expectations of what would or could happen, as well as fill her day with what simply made her feel most like herself, she remained focused on her pursuit. She also overcame the anxiety and fear regarding changing her path (quitting grad school), in addition to the uncertainty of then leaving her part-time publishing job (although becoming a published author kept her in this industry).

Her commitment to doing what she does because she loves doing it has even allowed her to help her husband pursue his own dream of opening a restaurant— which occurred in 2009. And if you're wondering how she met him, a fan of Orangette referred him to the blog, and things took off from there.

Neither becoming a best-selling author nor meeting her future husband was a goal of Molly's when she embarked on this journey, but remaining focused had a funny way of producing these results all the same.

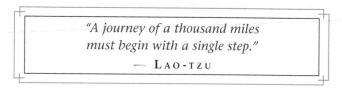

> *"A journey of a thousand miles*
> *must begin with a single step."*
> — LAO-TZU

Total Commitment

Often when we set a goal for ourselves—be it completing graduate school, starting a business, or learning how to speak another language—we conceive an idea of how long it should take and what we'll get out of it when we're done. We find ourselves concerned about how others perceive us, filtering the inundation of information inherent to living in the 21st century and constantly updating our Facebook status.

The third element of the Adventure in Everything system is *total commitment*. As I stated in the Introduction, this is the pursuit of an endeavor with flexibility about its execution, detachment from its results, and complete and total focus on the task at hand. If I went to grad school and invested all of my energy worrying about how long it would take me to finish the degree, rather than focusing on gaining a fundamental understanding of the course material, then I'd be exhibiting little flexibility in how I conducted myself. If I were working toward this degree only because of the opportunities I expected to have afterward, then I'd not only be setting myself up for disappointment if my expectations weren't met, but I'd have little energy left to actually enjoy the process of learning. And if I decided to just play video games instead of study, then I wouldn't be getting the most out of my degree—if I were able to earn one at all.

In contrast, Molly set out to attend grad school and start her blog because she simply wanted to participate in activities that helped her feel most like herself—not because she was hung up on what she was going to get out of them. Had she been a student at one of my workshops, she would have needed less help in applying this element to her life than other people.

Initially, Molly pursued her doctorate to enjoy a program that gave her an opportunity to learn. However, when it no longer served her, she let it go. She didn't give herself a set amount of time in which to earn the degree, her interest in anthropology wasn't contingent on whether or not she got a cushy university job when she graduated, and she certainly wasn't fixated on how cool it would be to put a fancy title alongside her name.

It was her total commitment to school that, ironically enough, prompted her to leave. It was her awareness of the task at hand that helped her realize that instead of studying the French social-security system, she wanted to think and write about food. Again, when she started Orangette, Molly most likely didn't consider that this blog could be her ticket to becoming a food columnist or a best-selling author. She just spent some of each day writing about roasted cauliflower, Parisian flan, and heirloom-tomato sandwiches . . . and loved every moment of it. Total commitment to anthropology caused her to no longer want to pursue her Ph.D., and her total commitment to writing about food helped her make her dreams come true.

Your first task in developing a total commitment to your own endeavors is to think of one you've pursued in which you exhibited qualities similar to Molly's when she started writing her blog. Consider the following questions:

- What classes did you take in school that you completely and totally loved?

- Are there workshops you've attended or specific skills you've learned that you became completely and totally immersed in finding out more about?

- What part-time job have you worked at "just to have a little fun," but which deep down you knew was something you had a passion for?

- Which of your hobbies have you always wished you could somehow build a career on?

In your journal, jot down these questions, and then respond in a stream-of-consciousness fashion for at least 15 minutes. When you've come up with at least one endeavor, spend some more time noting how you felt while performing whatever tasks it required of you. Once you've done all of this, put the journal aside.

The remainder of this chapter will teach you how to develop the ability to make a total commitment to whatever you choose to pursue in your life. In a sense, it will show you how to focus on the process of achieving your goals rather than their results. The primary components of making a total commitment to your pursuits are *flexibility, detachment,* and *focus,* but before explaining how to cultivate these qualities, I'll take you through a process that will help you become the most secure and confident version of yourself possible. This happens when you identify your strengths.

> *To make a total commitment is to acknowledge*
> *your goal and work with whatever*
> *comes up in the moment.*

Identify Your Strengths

Chris began her career as a clerk at the front desk of a hotel. The hotel was part of the Marriott International chain, and although the job was part-time and only earned her an hourly wage, she accepted it as a way to enter the workforce upon finishing school. She didn't have any particular aspirations to move up in the company, but she took her responsibilities seriously, regularly incorporated her supervisors' feedback to improve her performance, and was quickly offered a full-time position.

Twenty-three years later, Chris is a regional vice president.

Of course, many things happened over the course of her time with the company. As she worked her way up from the front desk to management, Chris paid close attention to how she solved problems and accomplished tasks. Eventually, she realized that her particular abilities and interests would be better utilized in revenue management. Applying a unique problem-solving method that she'd discovered in customer service, Chris was able to maximize the potential of her group and formulate strategies for improving her region's bottom line. Her continual rise through the corporate ranks caused her to become passionate about how people can harness their natural gifts. Eventually, she began developing and using certain concepts to make decisions about how to build her teams and which tasks she assigned to different individuals.

Chris's philosophy was simple: people in the workplace are inclined to be more engaged, have more energy, and experience greater self-awareness when they have jobs that utilize their natural talents. She had employees complete a Gallup's StrengthsFinder assessment, as well as a survey that she designed, to reveal what their strengths were. The results were as expected, in that her employees really were more interested, energized, and appreciative on the job when they were doing what they were good at. Fortunately, the higher-ups at Marriott not only saw that Chris was worthy of the eventual promotion to vice president, but they gave her room to find creative ways to expand this philosophy to other areas of the company. When

I had the chance to meet Chris, she'd started work on a strengths-based team to be utilized throughout her region and was in the process of putting together a ten-week online leadership course to be used by Marriott employees throughout the world.

Whether working at a job, raising a family, or pursuing another interest, all of us stand to benefit from Chris's story and the work she's done at her company. We each have an opportunity to either aspire to new endeavors or continue working in our current circumstances with total commitment.

However, totally committing to something is a difficult task, as we may feel we're unqualified or, as I discussed in Element #2, fear the unknown. Making a total commitment when we're hung up on our perceived shortcomings or unsure of ourselves is nearly impossible, and we generally have the chance to shape our goals around the natural strengths we bring to the table. As Chris's experience shows, going after something we desire using our natural strengths can help us engage in the process, feel energized as we accomplish tasks, and become more self-aware along the way. These are the fundamental qualities of one who has total commitment.

So how do you identify and capitalize on your strengths? An entire book could be written on this subject—and many already have been—but for the purposes of conveying this idea to you, I'd like to present a few simple ways. When working with her employees, Chris utilizes the Gallup's StrengthsFinder assessment and a survey to identify in which areas they feel most like themselves.

An alternative to taking an assessment is to conduct an interview with friends or family members you trust, asking them what they feel your natural strengths are and for when those attributes were apparent. Then make an evaluation based on their feedback. To give you a start, I've listed many different positive qualities that a person can exhibit while pursuing an endeavor:

Determination	Wisdom	Focus
Creativity	Imagination	Nurturing
Conscientiousness	Precision	Analysis
Computation	Leadership	Courage
Authority	Charm	Daring
Thoroughness	Fastidiousness	Theatricality
Inventiveness	Candor	Resourcefulness

Conviction	Passion	Tenderness
Warmth	Compassion	Devotion
Elegance	Showmanship	Composure
Gregariousness	Organization	Discernment
Taste	Insight	Patience
Generosity	Ingenuity	Clarity

Your task is to consider the academic subjects, hobbies, and other activities that you identified earlier in this chapter as ones you completely and totally loved and ask yourself which of the above qualities you exhibited while engaged in these pursuits. In your journal, write down the characteristics you feel you've displayed.

Ultimately, though, one very simple way of identifying your strengths is to look at this list, or any organized list of personality types, and figure out what you bring to your endeavors by reflecting on which qualities help you feel particularly enthusiastic about what you do. Once you come to some conclusions, you'll be on your way to discovering which aspects of your character will ground you while you're making a total commitment.

> *For some people, discovering their gifts becomes more of a marathon than a sprint.*

Flexibility, Detachment, and Focus

It took Chris a while to develop insights into her own strengths and abilities, and Molly spent a number of years in higher education before she realized that she didn't actually want to be immersed in that world. I was a mountain guide for several years before I created a vision for how to take my own work to a more fulfilling level. Identifying and capitalizing on your positive attributes is often a long-term process, and taking a dozen assessment tests and doing 20 hours of stream-of-consciousness writing may still not give you a precise idea of your best qualities.

This is okay. As we've already explored in Element #2, a major part of seeking adventure in all aspects of our lives is not knowing how something is going to turn out in the end. This can be applied to finding our strengths as well; and whether we discover ours in a half hour or a half century, working toward doing so will help us develop greater self-awareness as we move forward.

When we possess a heightened sense of self-worth and are in control of our behavior in response to various situations, we're better prepared to solve problems and accomplish our goals. If identifying what we're good at helps ground us and establishes an awareness of what we bring to our pursuits, then we can further cultivate that understanding through greater flexibility, detachment, and focus along the way. As I've previously mentioned, exhibiting these three qualities will help clarify our total commitment to an aspiration by enabling us to enjoy the ride rather than fixate on the finish line. I'll elaborate on these three qualities in the sections that follow.

Be Flexible in Execution

In the Introduction, we explored the concept of the beginner's mind. Recall that the example of this concept was going to an oil-painting workshop and fully embracing all possibilities of what could happen. We also examined how we might refuse to attend the class due to a fear of not being good enough—feeling that we've never previously been comfortable in such a novel situation, so that's how it will always be. Too often, we decide against leaving our comfort zone for the sake of new opportunities because they might disrupt our worldview—and having such a disturbance would be scary and confusing. Instead, we fall into the pattern of saying no to new and different experiences.

A habit is unconsciously doing something based on previous behaviors that produced favorable outcomes. You might have made the right decision when you turned down the chance to study painting, for your perceived shortcomings in such an area would have destroyed your grade point average. Maybe your school had a close-minded teacher who taught only one approach to this subject and would have provided you with the poor experience you feared. Therefore, you formed the habit of avoiding more creative pursuits.

An integral aspect of practicing total commitment is being flexible in how you go about seeking an endeavor. Using your beginner's mind, let's say that you finally decide to attend the oil-painting workshop to see what happens. Perhaps you're particularly analytical and precise in how you do things. As a result, you initially struggle to participate in the most elementary still-life painting exercise because the teacher's directions ask you to be fluid and imaginative, something you're not comfortable with. By embracing flexibility while taking part in the workshop, you forsake getting flustered or upset by these challenges, and instead ask the instructor for help. He or she then comes over, looks at you, looks at your effort, and recommends that you draw a grid on your canvas in order to utilize your precise nature (*ahem,* capitalizing on your strengths) and render the still life in a far less loosey-goosey way. Even though you see everyone else having success with the apparently imaginative and flowing process that was originally suggested, you embrace flexibility in how you execute the endeavor for yourself. This only happens when you slow down, consider your options, and, as is the case in this example, seek support.

Now, consider this concept of flexibility in relation to the endeavors you reflected on in your journal at the beginning of Element #3. When you pursued that class/workshop/hobby/job, did you feel that you had the license to go about it in the way you wanted? Did you make it your own? If not, what might you do differently now to better emulate this behavior? Spend some time exploring these questions in your journal before moving on to the following section.

Detach from Results

At the end of the workshop, you receive great accolades from the instructor, an art agent comes by the school and takes you on as a client, and you sell out your first-ever gallery showing in a matter of hours.

And then you wake up.

Of course, outside of a Judy Garland or Barbra Streisand film, this kind of rags-to-riches scenario rarely plays itself out. While there are some lucky individuals who, through a combination of ability and chance, do experience such a rapid rise to fame, the rest of us tend to see more modest and gradual developments.

Although it would be quite pleasant for you to receive high praise from your instructor and attain the level of success described above, attending the workshop out of a desire to reap the fantastic rewards you imagine for yourself completely undermines your ability to make a total commitment to the endeavor itself. How many people do you know who work at high-powered jobs that earn them a lot of money and fancy amenities, but who seem to be miserable and allow work to suck their souls right out of them? If they really are unhappy, then they're most likely in these positions only for the results of their efforts—in this case, the salary—not because they actually enjoy what they do.

During my climbing expeditions, I often encounter individuals who feel success is a must and that their self-worth is tied to an outcome—for instance, they'll consider themselves a failure if they don't make it to the top of the mountain. In response, I have them slow down by breathing in between each move in order to notice the texture and shape of each hand- and foothold. When they reach the top, I ask them to reflect on how this new approach to accomplishing a task might impact how they deal with every other aspect of their lives. Invariably, they imagine that this new method will help them enrich their daily existence, so they set an intention to take a bit more pleasure in each moment . . . and many succeed in doing just that.

Whether it's participating in an oil-painting workshop for the sake of enjoying the smell of linseed oil or climbing a mountain just to see the birds flying closer to you, such gems won't ever cross your path until you separate yourself from the end product. Like you did in the previous section, take some time right now to write in your journal, and determine whether you detached from the results when you were having a good time with the endeavor you explored at the beginning of this chapter.

Focus on the Task at Hand

So let's say that you're at the oil-painting workshop and you've used the beginner's mind to embrace the idea that anything is possible, you've let go of certain preconceived ideas of how you must participate, and you've detached from what may or may not happen as a result of being there. What, then, is left for you to do?

Once all of this has occurred, your job, quite simply, is to paint. If you're meticulous and analytical when you do so, then great. *Just paint.* If you've relaxed enough to let go of the vision of one day selling your work at a gallery, that's perfect. *Just paint.* Use your precision to experiment with ultramarine and crimson to find the deepest shade of purple you can. Center your attention and think of nothing else but the brush, the paint, and the canvas. *Just paint.*

Now, concentrating on the task at hand can, of course, be applied to all situations. When you're filing papers at work, focus on your job instead of simultaneously gossiping with the person in the cubicle next to you. While you're reading a book to your children, don't check your BlackBerry to see if a co-worker has delivered a report that you need for a meeting the next morning. And when you're climbing a mountain, give your full attention to *the mountain.* Even though most people who participate in my expeditions don't need a reminder to remain focused on this particular task, it's worth noting that many of them go on to apply that same dedication to whatever they do as they move on with their lives. Suddenly, having more followers on Twitter isn't quite as important.

Recall in the Introduction when I had you put down the book and zero in on nothing but your breath for 15 seconds. Do you remember how difficult that was? While this level of concentration can be applied to all efforts, it can take a long time to develop this skill. Returning to this technique can be very helpful in increasing your ability to maintain focus. Additionally, you can explore the following exercise, which will help you integrate flexibility and detachment as well.

> *We have the greatest impact when we let*
> *go of trying to make an impact.*

The U-Turn Exercise

Cultivating greater self-awareness to the point of being more flexible, detached, and focused can be a lengthy process. If being totally mindful of the task at hand were such an easy thing to do, everyone would be doing it and we'd never hear stories about people who caused car accidents because they were texting, talking, and rummaging through their glove compartments while attempting to drive. Although the general lesson of embodying these three qualities is to take the time to reflect on your reactions, behaviors, and habits while pursuing a goal, this U-turn exercise can give you a jump start in including Element #3: Total Commitment in your Adventure in Everything experiment.

This activity asks you to respond to a difficult challenge in a way that's the opposite of what's expected. For example, perhaps you're a manager at a customer-service center, and your particular management style only allows you to determine how to process customer feedback: you design the comment forms, you tell your employees how to respond to hostility, and you make any decisions about what changes need to be made. Although it can sometimes be stressful and demanding, this seems to work well because you can keep everything under control and you're able to capitalize on your take-charge attitude.

But when your company is suddenly overloaded with calls because of a product defect, it quickly becomes clear that you're going to dig yourself an early grave if you continue to absorb all the weight of the situation yourself. With significant pressure from your superiors to step up and accommodate the high volume of customer requests, you realize that your unilateral way of doing things isn't feasible.

So in applying the U-turn exercise to this problem, you decide to reach out and ask your employees for their feedback and modify things based on what they say. Earlier in this chapter you read how making a total commitment to a task can allow you to stay grounded by first capitalizing on your strengths. Well, you're still utilizing your leadership qualities in managing your team, but you're doing so in the *opposite* way.

This technique can be applied to nonwork situations as well. I lead many different types of people through my climbing expeditions, but there are two in particular who appear quite frequently. The first group, which I mentioned a few pages ago, includes the individuals who qualify their successes and self-worth by whether or not they make it to the top.

The other type is disconnected from outcomes to such an extent that they give themselves permission to fail and are uncomfortable with achieving success because it could mean unwelcome change. In climbing, they might not have the ability to envision reaching the summit, instead wishing to return to the bottom as soon as it becomes remotely challenging. Generally, they may exhibit a disconnection from their job, relationships, and all other endeavors that have the potential to slightly push them past their own boundaries.

My response to both groups of people is to prescribe the U-turn exercise. For the driven people, I instruct them to slow down, breathe, and take note of their surroundings. With disconnected individuals, I prepare them at the bottom of the mountain to visualize their path to the top, have them imagine what a new way of being might be like, and ask them for permission to remind them of this new way of being if they should encounter challenges while climbing. In each instance, the climber develops an understanding of what their typical response to a challenge is and why.

To complete this exercise, consider an issue in your life: a difficult work situation, your fear of taking a risk, or maybe a disagreement with a spouse or family member. Then write the concern down in your journal, along with any solutions that are representative of how you'd normally respond to it. Next, create a list of options that demonstrates different ways of approaching the problem. Once you've decided on a method, go ahead and apply it.

If you find that brainstorming in your journal hasn't produced effective results, go back to the people you interviewed to help you identify your strengths, see if they'll give you 30 more minutes of their time, and find out what they feel your typical way of responding to a situation might be and what qualifies as the opposite of that behavior.

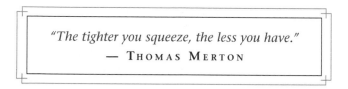

> *"The tighter you squeeze, the less you have."*
> — THOMAS MERTON

Making a Total Commitment Begins Now

In reading this chapter, you might have noticed a potential paradox in how one might pursue a total commitment. The first part of the process is to identify and capitalize on your strengths—that is, to work at being completely true to who you are. The second part is to foster greater flexibility, detachment, and focus; and with the help of the U-turn exercise, to strive to do the opposite of what you've done before.

While these components might seem to contradict each other, they're intended to serve two sides of the same basic objective: making a total commitment. Molly the blogger had a natural ability to learn, and did so in both her scholarly and writing endeavors, but letting go of her academic aspirations ushered in a flexibility and detachment in how she explored her interest in food. In the customer-service example, you capitalized on your strengths as a leader in both situations, but went about fulfilling that role in a way that was the opposite of what was expected.

In the initial phase of making a total commitment, ground yourself in what you do best. Then explore the different ways in which that commitment can take shape. Making a total commitment isn't about remaining in a fixed mind-set, but about changing your path in the spirit of reaching your goal. It begins *now*.

Total-Commitment Task List

- Consider past endeavors that you found particularly satisfying, and write in a stream-of-consciousness fashion in your journal to explore why you found them so enjoyable.

- Pick qualities from the list of strengths and engage trusted companions in conversations to analyze your personality traits and what you bring to various tasks and situations.

- In your journal, examine the concepts of flexibility and detachment from results as they relate to the past endeavors you cited earlier in this chapter.

■ Conduct the U-turn exercise in relation to a challenge or struggle in your life, and use your journal and trusted companions as tools for finding opposite ways of behaving.

ELEMENT #4

TOLERANCE FOR ADVERSITY

By the time I turned 20, I'd already climbed my way to the top of a fair number of mountains. I'd reached the high-altitude peaks of Mexico and Ecuador, conquered dozens of summits in Washington State, and had even spent a few days living on the side of El Capitan in Yosemite. I was so confident in my ability to accomplish whatever climbing goals I set for myself that it seemed like a good idea to join my friend Andy on a trip up to the Ruth Gorge.

The Ruth Gorge was no ordinary climbing area—and our main objective was an icy fortress named Moose's Tooth. Twice the height of El Capitan, this Alaskan monster was far enough north that we would experience 24 hours of daylight when we arrived during the heart of summer. Although Andy and I were young, we felt that the variety of ice and rock climbs we'd both done had prepared us for whatever challenges awaited— and we weren't the only ones with such confidence. Earlier that year, we'd received a generous grant from The American Alpine Club to explore and ascend new climbs in the Ruth Gorge.

Our campsite was so remote that after arriving at Anchorage International Airport, we drove north for three hours and then had to take a single-engine plane to our base camp. On this flight, we had to use hand gestures, as we couldn't hear ourselves or the pilot over the engine's noise. For the duration of our time in the air, we pointed out the many mountains and terrains that we recognized from pictures as a way to demonstrate how ridiculously psyched we were to be on this adventure. Fortunately, though, this last leg of the journey was only an hour long.

Perhaps it was the shock of going from incessant noise to complete quiet, or maybe it was the alarm we felt at arriving in a winter wonderland in the middle of summer, but as we stood there only moments after the pilot had left, surveying the pristine serenity of the surrounding landscape and looking up at the *tens of thousands of feet* we were about to climb, I started to get a weird feeling.

"What have we gotten ourselves into?" I asked my partner.

"We've gotten ourselves into Alaska, Matt. It's not that hard, you know."

"Yes, thank you."

"There's no immigration or anything . . ."

"I know."

". . . because it's part of the United States."

I waited for my friend to be finished with his bit of comedy before we went about pitching the tent and setting up camp.

□ □

Once everything was organized and we'd sorted through our 200 pounds of stuff, we set out for the mountain. It was a struggle. Andy took his turn to lead, then I took mine. Sometimes we took an hour-long break, sometimes we took two. Sometimes we wondered why we'd put ourselves in such an extreme situation, and sometimes we took a moment to enjoy the most gorgeous landscape either of us had ever seen. Sometimes a day would fly by because Andy made quick use of his wicked sense of humor and we spent the whole day laughing, and sometimes we just worked in total silence. For the entire 20 days that we climbed, I felt more fulfilled and content than I ever had before.

Well . . . not exactly. In fact, none of the events in the previous paragraph ever happened. We didn't climb a single foot of Moose's Tooth. After saving up money, organizing all the gear, and preparing ourselves mentally for what was going to be the biggest climb of our lives, it snowed and rained every day we were there. We were stranded with nothing but a tent for shelter, had no ability to travel any great distances, and couldn't get picked up because there wasn't anywhere for the plane to land.

Actually, the only true statement in the entire paragraph is that Andy really does have a wicked sense of humor. Oh yeah, and that this experience really did last for 20 days.

Consider what it would be like to sit in a 35-square-foot tent with another person for 20 days. What would you do? Would you talk about every topic you could think of ad nauseam? We did. Would you read every piece of written material you had, including the labels on food packages? We did. Would you strap on your snowshoes and walk 100 yards and back because that was as far as you could go without risking your safety? We did. At one point, I even found myself staring at Andy while he was reading.

"What are you doing?" he asked me.

"I'm watching you," I replied.

"I'm reading."

"I know. And I'm watching you read," I said.

"Why?" he questioned.

"I don't know. I wish there was something better for me to do, though."

Andy seemed to ponder that for a second. Then he put down the book and stared back at me.

"What are *you* doing?" The game had begun.

"I'm watching you," he challenged.

"Why?"

"Well, you seemed to think it was so great just a moment ago. Have you matured so much in the last 20 seconds that this is no longer totally awesome?"

"No . . ."

Andy continued: "I thought it was a game: *who can be the creepiest watch-the-other-guy-in-the tent guy for the longest amount of time?*"

I snorted.

"I think you could win this one, Matt. You're really creepy . . ."

I laughed.

"And you're already in a tent . . ."

"Stop!" I said between chuckles.

"Stop laughing, Matt. You have to stare at me for no reason at all; otherwise, you won't win. And then your life as you know it will end. You were born to play this game. *You can do it.*"

We didn't even just play games that Andy invented to give me a hard time. We found scrap paper and made ourselves a chess set and a backgammon board. We did everything we could to make this situation as palatable as possible. Whenever I started a sentence with "I wish . . ." as in "I wish the snow would stop," my climbing partner shot back some sort of quip that brought me back to the present and ended my pity party. As soon as I started a sentence with "I just . . ." as in "I just want to get out of here," Andy would find yet another way to use small pieces of paper to create another form of entertainment that resembled something made by Parker Brothers.

The snow finally stopped. The rain stopped. But the pilot had to wait for the terrain to clear so he could land, and it took a couple of days of good weather to make this possible. In the end, we didn't climb a single foot; and all of the preparations, plans, and resources it took to make this trip happen wound up being unnecessary as we conducted our epic but involuntary experiment with seclusion.

But I wouldn't trade it for anything.

Even though I never got to follow Andy's lead in climbing the Ruth Gorge, sharing this experience with him and following his "lead" through creepy-guy staring contests and homemade chess sets planted a seed in me that took very little time to germinate. Out of these circumstances, I came to realize the importance of building tolerance for adverse situations. Making jokes for days on end in a snow-covered tent helped me understand how to laugh in the face of tough times. Allowing myself to let go of the climb taught me to take more risks—for even if things don't turn out how I want them to, I always have the ability to work as hard as I can. And I'll never forget the story of how I stared at my friend while he was reading because I really couldn't think of anything better to do.

After returning from Alaska, I decided to chart a different course for my life. Six months later, I landed the assistant-guide job in Chile that I mentioned in Element #2. Had I not developed a tolerance for adversity during those 20 days at the bottom of the Ruth Gorge, the Adventure in Everything system would never have been created.

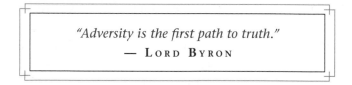

"Adversity is the first path to truth."
— LORD BYRON

Tolerance for Adversity

Adversity is an instance of misfortune that leads to a challenge and, in most cases, the distress that accompanies it. In other words, when we run into difficulty, our typical response is to think that life sucks.

However we define it, adversity is something that each of us encounters every day. If we run out of gas on the highway, it pops up as we curse ourselves for not planning our travels properly. If we injure ourselves while going for a run or playing football, we resent our inability to handle the rigors of a physically active lifestyle. Or if we get passed over for a promotion at work, we experience it when we feel unappreciated and undervalued by our employer. We grapple with these and countless other adverse situations as we're challenged to accomplish our goals.

For most people, any type of adversity causes a stressful response, with a number of negative emotions, such as anger, worry, and grief. Once these feelings surface, they play out in counteractive ways—for example, rejecting all forms of physical activity in response to getting injured or quitting the job that didn't offer a promotion. Then, once they've exhausted every bad feeling they can, they're left unemployed, sedentary, or in whatever situation was created by their unproductive choices. Individuals who allow adversity to define them are likely to feel less fulfilled, be offered fewer opportunities, and have a generally distasteful reaction to whatever happens to them. In short, their lives really do suck.

Element #4 of the Adventure in Everything system is *tolerance for adversity.* You've likely already figured out that this concept is defined by your ability to work past adversity without succumbing to the distress and negativity that's typically associated with it. When you develop a tolerance for adversity, you accept what you can't control, and adapt to it, while still exercising the power to change what's within your circle of influence. My experience at the Ruth Gorge demonstrates how successfully working past adversity—in this case, embracing the humor and absurdity of traveling to Alaska only to spend three weeks in a tent—can positively impact one's life. Upon overcoming the challenges inherent in that situation, I had the courage and conviction to leave my job and become an assistant guide on a climbing expedition. Ultimately, as things got more interesting, that circle of influence grew.

> *Challenge and difficulty are one thing.*
> *Stress is another.*

Why Is Tolerance for Adversity Important?

It may sound nice that I further developed the ability to take risks as a result of my experience with Andy, but why should tolerance for adversity be such a significant ingredient in finding Adventure in Everything? Why do people who don't possess this trait feel less fulfilled and have fewer opportunities? Difficulties and challenges are inherent in life, and we have no control over how or when they occur. What we do have command of, though, is whether or not we will feel stress, or any of the previously mentioned negative emotions that accompany it.

Those who succumb to such stress probably won't enjoy life's small moments as much, making them less likely to feel gratification. If you had a boss who was constantly yelling at you, then it would be far more conceivable that you might hate your job if you always took this behavior as a personal attack. Maybe you'd even spend your downtime thinking of ways you'd like to scream in his or her face when you finally win the lottery and no longer need that job.

Likewise, those who succumb to stress are more likely to run away from the situations that trigger it, thus affording themselves fewer opportunities to succeed in their endeavors. If, after another bout of yelling, you decide to tell off your direct superior and quit on the spot, you've not only burned whatever bridges you may have built during your time with that company, but you've cut out the possibility of better things happening in that environment. What if your boss was about to be fired and the president was planning to offer you a promotion to fill the vacancy? What if a small group of employees in your department was thinking of starting a company, and because you were thought of as a stable and reliable worker, they wanted to take you along? Neither of these opportunities would be open to you if you allowed your stress to dictate your actions.

This is not to say that to develop a tolerance for adversity is to accept any problems you encounter and put up with awful circumstances indefinitely. If the position with the screaming boss is absolutely essential at this point in time, in that it's the only one close to home that offers the health insurance you need to keep your family covered, then it might be necessary to remain there for a while.

However, you probably could find another opportunity with comparable benefits; and developing a tolerance for the situation would permit you to make more measured, professional decisions. For example, you could let your boss yell at you, go back to your desk, do your work, search for a new job in your free time, and then give the proper notice when you find something better. No bridges have been burned in this scenario, which gives you the chance to either return to the company one day or work with former co-workers in a different capacity. More important, knowing that you took the high road will likely be far more fulfilling than a series of inappropriate expletives directed toward someone who probably just needs a hug in a bad way.

How does one go from wanting to tell off his or her boss to taking more even-tempered actions? The following section will show you a way to assess your own patterns of responding to adversity, and the remainder of Element #4 will then teach you how to use this information to help build a tolerance for situations that reflect these patterns.

> *The human experience is pretty ridiculous.*
> *It helps to recognize that.*

The Tolerance-for-Adversity Self-Assessment

In any given day, there are just as many opportunities to experience adversity as there are minutes. After all, difficult situations can show up in all aspects of life and in countless ways. The following exercise is a self-assessment where you'll be presented with a series of categories that reflect different facets of everyday existence. Each one will have components that may be a source of adversity, as well as examples of specific circumstances that have the potential to become stressful.

Your task is to go through these various categories (in bold and italics) and components (in bold), and then, as honestly as you can, choose the situations that you feel are most likely to be sources of stress and write them down in your journal. If you don't feel you relate to any of the options, and as such don't consider that component to be an area of tension, you're welcome to pass over it and move on to the next one. Go ahead and do this now.

Family/Relationships

Marriage/Romance

a. I don't have anyone special in my life, and this continues to be a source of pain for me.

b. My relationship has many problems, and I sometimes wonder if I should simply get out of it.

c. I've just begun seeing someone, but there are several things about him/her that leave me feeling wary about the prospects of this relationship.

Immediate Family Members

    a.   My parents drive me crazy. It's as simple as that.

    b.   I wish I had a closer relationship with my siblings.

    c.   I've lost one or more of my immediate family members, and I still haven't gotten over it.

Close Friends

    a.   My closest friends don't live nearby, and I hardly ever see them.

    b.   I don't really have many close friends, and I'm not sure why.

    c.   I love some of my close friends very much, but more often than not they get on my nerves.

Friendly Acquaintances

    a.   I like the various people in my life just fine, but I don't really have that much in common with them.

    b.   I'd like to meet new people, but I tend to be too shy to put myself out there.

    c.   I'm tired of the same old parties with the same old conversations happening over and over again.

Business/Professional

Business Ownership

    a.   I've always wanted to have my own business, but I don't seem to have the courage to make it happen.

    b.   I've tried to make my business work, but I can't ever seem to get ahead of the game.

    c.   My business has completely taken over my life, and I don't ever have time for my family and friends.

Current Job

    a.   I hate my job.

    b.   My boss constantly picks on me and yells at me for no reason.

    c.   My job is okay, but there's no room for growth.

Career Planning

    a.   I really have no idea what I want to do with my life.

    b.   I know what I want to do for a living, but my current obligations have made it impossible for me to make it happen.

c. I keep working toward making my dream career a reality, but I don't seem to be making any progress.

Education

a. I know what I'd like to do with my life, but I don't have the money to pay for the necessary education to make it happen.

b. The programs I'm interested in aren't located nearby, and I can't relocate.

c. I don't have the best academic history, and it will be tough to convince schools of my promise as a student.

Personal Finance

Income

a. I'm broke, and I always will be.

b. Based on my salary, it seems that I'm making enough money, but I always seem to go through it like water.

c. I always feel as if I count on others to help me squeak by, and I want my independence.

Debt

    a.   The balances on my credit cards are getting out of control.

    b.   All of my money seems to go toward my mortgage and car payment, and there's nothing left over as disposable income.

    c.   I may have to default on a loan, and my credit rating is about to be completely rocked.

Short-term Goals

    a.   I know that I need to scale back my month-to-month spending, but I can't seem to budget properly.

    b.   My car is falling apart, and I can't afford to get a new one right now.

    c.   My income is fine for scraping by, but I'm never able to branch out and do anything new because I can't afford to.

Long-term Goals

    a.   I've been paying rent for years. I want to buy my own place, but just can't afford a down payment.

    b.   I'm not putting away anything for my retirement, and I'm very uncomfortable with this.

    c.   My means are just above the limit to qualify for financial aid for my children's educations, and I don't know what to do.

Lifestyle

Diet

    a.   My diet is awful. There's no denying it.

    b.   People are always recommending the newest dieting fad to me, but I don't really know how I should be eating.

    c.   I want to buy organic foods and eat more healthfully, but I really can't afford to do so.

Physical Activity

    a.   No matter how many books, videos, and gym memberships I get, I can't seem to inspire myself to stay in shape.

    b.   I'm tired of the same old exercise routines.

    c.   I'd like to be more physically active by taking up a sport, but I don't really know anyone who would want to join me.

Recreation

a. I never have time for leisure. The busyness of my life keeps me from enjoying such things.

b. There are certain activities I enjoy, but I don't know anyone who also likes to participate in them.

c. I know I should set aside more time for recreation, but I have no idea what activities would be appropriate for me.

Hobbies

a. With each new year, I resolve to find a hobby . . . but I never do.

b. I don't have hobbies. Hobbies are for nerds who are the stars of the local Renaissance festival.

c. I can't afford the hobby that I want to pursue.

Health

Weight

a. I can't ever seem to get my weight under control.

b. I would love to do a Lap-Band procedure, but my insurance won't cover it.

    c.   It's unfair that I seem to only have to look at food to gain weight, while my siblings are all thin.

Short-term Illness

    a.   I always seem to have a cold or some other type of annoying illness.

    b.   I have an infection, and the antibiotics are wreaking havoc on my digestive system.

    c.   I injured myself, and my life is pretty much going to suck for the next six weeks.

Chronic Conditions

    a.   I haven't had a good night's sleep since I was a kid.

    b.   No matter what I do, my back always seems to hurt.

    c.   My allergies are driving me crazy.

Disease

    a.   I was diagnosed with an incurable disease, and it feels as if my life is over.

    b.   Given what's out there, I'm constantly afraid of catching something.

c. My partner has been diagnosed with a medical condition, and I have no idea what to do.

Spiritual Growth

Religion

a. I want to practice my religion, but I disagree with so many of its tenets.

b. I'm still recovering from the dogma I was subjected to as a child.

c. I feel that all organized religions distort the pursuit of truth.

Personal Ritual

a. I want to have some sort of spiritual practice, but I don't know what it should be.

b. I have a hard time finding good information about the spiritual path I'd like to pursue.

c. It's difficult to maintain the discipline to practice on a daily basis.

Community

a. I love my religion, but I can't find the right place to practice it.

b. Religious people drive me nuts, and I want nothing to do with them.

c. My spiritual practice requires me to pursue it in isolation, but I'd also like to take part in related discussions or forums.

Purpose

a. I don't believe in anything, and it makes me feel empty inside.

b. I do what learned people tell me to do, but it still leaves me unfulfilled.

c. I wish I felt better about what it means to be alive.

Now that you've gone through the entire assessment, take a look at the situations that you related to and wrote down. They each describe a stress-based reaction, or what may lead to one; and by putting them in your journal, you're identifying them as a source of tension. This assessment isn't intended to provide you with an involved psychological profile or be a general comment on your personality traits; it's only supposed to help you pinpoint circumstances and issues that trigger negative, unproductive responses.

How can this assessment be applied as you build your tolerance for adversity? As you work on the exercises in the following two sections, you'll be presented with opportunities to reflect on your own obstacles and challenges. You can use any of the situations that you made note of in your journal to establish a specific aspect of your life that needs to be explored. In other words, determining that you feel angst toward religion or frustration over always being broke will be valuable information as you build your tolerance for adversity in practical ways.

> *Self-discipline shows an ability to tolerate stress without compromising values. It is something that we can practice and train ourselves to utilize.*

The Three Steps of Tolerance

Now that you've gone through the Tolerance-for-Adversity Self-Assessment, choose one of the situations that describes a reaction you've had in the past. Then, take a moment to remember a specific example of when you experienced stress related to that situation. Did you get mad at your friend for always being busy or not living close enough? Did you suppress all of your inner turmoil about how your parents made you go to church or synagogue? But then when they made a passing comment about how you should raise *your* children (who haven't even been born yet), you screamed at them? Returning to the example of the yelling boss, did you go to happy hour after work and have several drinks in response to how hard he or she was riding you that day?

As with many of the concepts in the Adventure in Everything system, entire books could be written on how to better tolerate adversity, and of course, quite a few already have been. To approach this with the goal of creating more adventure in your life, though, I'm going to introduce three basic steps to help you respond in a more relaxed way to an adverse situation: (1) *acknowledge* that it's a difficult one, (2) *reflect* on how you typically respond to it, and (3) *plan* for how to move forward in overcoming this obstacle.

Acknowledge

When adversity strikes, the first step is to simply recognize that it is in fact a difficult situation. In other words, when you lose your confidence due to a bad day at work, you're simply saying something to the effect of: "Oh, this is what Matt was talking about in Element #4." Even though it may seem like a particularly elementary action to take, identifying unfavorable circumstances helps you to shift your mind-set from *Poor me, this really sucks* to *What's next?* When you acknowledge adversity for what it is, you prepare yourself for a far more productive reaction—and you've taken this step just by writing down a situation from the assessment.

Reflect

Once you've asked yourself *What's next?* the next task is to actually reflect on your standard response. If you usually freak out when you get yelled at by your boss, then this is your time to become aware of that. To help yourself identify the nature of your typical reaction to stress, consider which of the following negative emotions you tend to feel:

- *Anger:* "I clench my teeth, punch the air, and then walk it off."

- *Fear:* "I avoid problematic experiences completely."

- *Worry:* "I fret, pace, and imagine a hundred different what-if scenarios."

- *Sadness:* "I experience the helpless sense of wishing things could be better."

- *Depression:* "I wind up completely inert, without any awareness of my own value."

- *Grief:* "I feel empty inside; nothing could ever make me whole again."

- *Lethargy:* "I feel heavy and unwilling to move forward in a positive way."

- *Irritability:* "I create boundaries all around me and snap at others."

- *Mania:* "I get completely overwhelmed and lose the ability to settle down."

Consider these emotions while actively thinking about your usual reaction to adversity. Alternatively, you can do 15 minutes of stream-of-consciousness writing about your normal response to one of the situations you wrote down from the self-assessment. Regardless of how you go about this process, the next time you have a problem, take a moment to reflect by allowing yourself to relate to the issue with greater objectivity.

Plan

What would happen if you went to college and there wasn't any sort of curriculum to follow in your pursuit of a degree? Or what if you didn't receive any specific instructions to adhere to when the doctor prescribed medicine for you? Without some type of structure, you're likely to make little progress in school, healing, or any other situation.

This is the importance of having a plan, and responding to adversity is no different. Once you've acknowledged that you're experiencing adversity and have reflected on how you usually react, it's time to form a strategy for moving forward. If your boss has been overly critical or condescending, address the concern with him or her directly, find a new job, or figure out some other productive way to respond to the problem. Once you create and then implement a plan, you've countered the adverse situation and rendered the stress and negative emotions unnecessary.

Practice the Three Steps

A simple way of training your mind to react to adversity is by describing what you typically do as soon as you encounter it. Open your journal and write out your own version of one of the situations you originally related to from the self-assessment exercise. It might read:

> *I haven't had a good night's sleep in five years.*

Choosing this particular issue is your way of acknowledging on paper that it's a problem (Step 1). Next, reflect on your normal reaction to this situation with the help of the previous bulleted list or a healthy dose of stream-of-consciousness writing (Step 2). If you choose to write, you might explore what could be causing your poor sleep, the nature of the advice you've received thus far, and your general feelings about the fact that this is happening. Last, create a different way to respond using a series of productive actions, which equates to creating a plan (Step 3). It may look like this:

Instead of lamenting my poor sleeping habits, I can consult with five health-care or therapeutic professionals and combine their feedback to resolve my problem in a systematic way.

You can do this for any other concerns from the self-assessment exercise, and also apply it to areas that I may not have covered. When you face such a situation again in the future, you'll be far more likely to react with tolerance, grace, and even humor.

Resilient people capitalize on opportunities.
Resilient people learn from all experiences.
Resilient people are adaptable to change.

Gabe, and Tolerance for Short- and Long-term Adversity

Gabe Rogel had a decision to make when he was 22 years old. After having completed the first of two years of photography school, he had a choice between working as a mountain-climbing guide, as he'd done the previous couple of summers, or landscaping and painting apartment complexes, as he'd done in high school. The position as a guide allowed him to pursue his love of climbing while traveling, camping . . . and getting paid; basically, it was his ideal summer job. If Gabe chose the other option, he'd be required to lift heavy rocks, toil in the hot sun, and perform menial tasks. He'd also have to live at home with his parents.

He chose to work for his father's landscaping company.

Leading up to this summer, Gabe hadn't simply finished one year of photography school. He'd also worked as a paid photographer. In his relatively short career, he'd already been fortunate enough to travel abroad, photographing anything that related to mountain climbing and outdoor recreation, as well as the most beautiful landscapes in the world. During this first year, he even sold some of his photos to companies like *Climbing* magazine and Patagonia and accumulated thousands of slides.

Gabe knew without a doubt that he wanted to do this work professionally, but he also knew that he was unlikely to find more than occasional success unless he got organized. He needed to catalog his slides, create lists of potential clients to submit photos to, and form the foundation of a legitimate business . . . and spending 15 hours a day, six days a week, as a climbing guide wasn't going to afford him this opportunity. In working for his father, Gabe had some hard, grueling days, but he also made time in the evenings and on weekends to set up his company. He spent as much time as he could numbering his slides, and he bribed his buddies with pizza so they'd come over and help.

Since that summer, Gabe has gone on to work for magazines such as *Men's Journal, National Geographic Adventure,* and *Time;* and has worked for clients such as Black Diamond Equipment and the United States government. He is, for all practical purposes, a rock star of his industry (**www.rogelphoto.com**).

Gabe's story could be applied to all elements of the Adventure in Everything system. It's been included here, though, because of how his decision to give up his ideal job put him in an adverse situation that he ultimately used in a productive way.

I explained earlier how not having tolerance for adversity can lead to feeling less fulfilled (a stress-based reaction to short-term adversity) and having fewer opportunities (a stress-based reaction to long-term adversity). Gabe was able to use the three steps to overcome short-term stress, even though he might not have consciously done so in the way I've laid out. When he was presented with an awfully large rock to haul, he might have noted that this work was tedious (acknowledge), recognized that he was doing it for a reason (reflect), and then took a moment to catch his breath and commit to at least one hour of cataloging photos that night (plan).

Similarly, Gabe very well could have applied the system in the longer term: he might have identified the need to give up his mountain-guide position (acknowledge), accepted that the sacrifice was necessary to accomplish his ultimate objective (reflect), and created a series of steps to take in order to get his business organized by the end of the summer (plan).

If he hadn't responded so productively to adversity, Gabe might not have become great at anything—and certainly not in a field as competitive as commercial photography. His story shows us that, in both the short and long term, we all have the opportunity to respond to adversity in a constructive way.

> *Tolerance for adversity is contagious when witnessed by others.*

Sometimes a poor reaction to adversity simply ruins our day, but then we're able to bounce back quickly. Sometimes a negative response has a much more significant effect, one in which it actually impinges on our ability to accomplish our goals and realize our dreams. Whether we experience a setback while driving and decide to solve our problem with grace, sacrifice a summer of excitement for the sake of something bigger, or simply laugh as much as possible while trapped in a tent for three weeks, developing a tolerance for adversity will help us have a more productive, enjoyable life.

Tolerance-for-Adversity Task List

- Complete the Tolerance-for-Adversity Self-Assessment.

- Reflect on one of the situations you related to in the self-assessment by either choosing emotional reactions you relate to from the list, or via 15 minutes of stream-of-consciousness writing in your journal.

■ Practice the three steps of *acknowledge, reflect,* and *plan* in relation to any of the situations you identified in the self-assessment. Use Gabe's story as an example of how you might respond to adversity in a productive way.

GREAT COMPANIONSHIP

Ronnie Dickson had to have surgery when he was 17. As a young boy, he was diagnosed with a condition known as Trevor's disease that caused a deformity in the growth plates of his left leg. The rest of his body grew and functioned normally, but this limb was misshapen and too short for walking and moving properly. Even though he had a leg-lengthening procedure in the third grade (which took an entire year), by ninth grade this leg forced him to walk on his toes in order to maintain proper balance. He was also in a lot of pain.

Ronnie was about to graduate from high school when he made the choice to have another surgery. Rather than attempt to elongate the leg again and go through dozens of procedures to *possibly* resolve what had been virtually a lifelong struggle, he decided to have his left leg amputated. This one surgery—not dozens—would take care of the issue.

It was an easy decision for him to make.

Ronnie had played soccer for many years as a child, but every time he participated in just one game, he couldn't walk until the following morning when he went to school. Still, the opportunity to step out on the field and show his competitive side for a little while was worth it. Once he had the surgery, though, he wasn't able to continue with the physically active lifestyle that he was used to due to the limitations of the standard, all-purpose prosthetic leg he was equipped with. This device enabled Ronnie to get around without crutches or any other support, but sports were out of the question.

One day soon after his procedure, he was in the waiting room of his prosthetist when he noticed an advertisement in a magazine for something called Extremity Games, which is an event similar to the X Games but which involves athletes with limb loss or limb differences. In reading about it, Ronnie learned that there was a whole series of sports that amputees participated in, such as kayaking, mountain biking, and even rock climbing. Was it really possible for him to get back into competitive sports?

A month after that office visit, Ronnie found an answer to that question . . . and then some. His girlfriend was participating in a half marathon, and he accompanied her to the registration tent, where vendors at the booths were offering information and giveaways. As she left to sign up, Ronnie noticed a table for an organization called Challenged Athletes Foundation (CAF). He went over to it and struck up a conversation with a man named Kelly.

Over the course of their conversation, Kelly explained that CAF specialized in helping athletes with special needs receive assistance that might otherwise be unavailable to them. Ronnie liked the idea of this group, but he didn't really consider himself an athlete anymore. Still, by the time they'd parted ways, Kelly and a CAF colleague named Lew had persuaded Ronnie to attempt a 5K race and, in their subsequent communications, convinced him that amputees had the ability to compete in sports.

Although he'd shown up at the race as his girlfriend's tagalong, Ronnie left that day a man with an invigorated spirit. He not only accepted Kelly's help and finished the 5K, but also participated in a triathlon, traveled to California and Oregon to find out more about new advancements in prosthetics, learned how to snowboard, and concurrently trained for the Extremity Games in the rock-climbing event.

Ronnie was also a beneficiary of help from various facilities that offered amputees advancing prosthetic technologies entering the marketplace. And now, still only in his early 20s, he works at one of those clinics.

It's probably important to point out that partway through his college career, Ronnie switched from being an English major to a prosthetics and orthotics major. And before even starting his senior year, he'd lined up a residency position designing prosthetics at a facility that provides free technology to 25 percent of its clients—many of whom receive prosthetics specially designed for the kinds of sports that Ronnie participates in.

There are many reasons why Ronnie's story is relevant to the Adventure in Everything system: his endeavors are high, his commitment is full, and his decision to have his left leg amputated epitomizes how one can embrace a situation with an uncertain outcome. However, I've included his story in this particular chapter for a different reason. Ronnie's transition from being a boy with a prosthetic leg to a man who competes in sports and designs prosthetics for a living shows that he has an abundance of something of particular value to his journey: great companionship.

> *Great companions help us find a life of*
> *authenticity, purpose, and inspiration.*

Who Are Our Great Companions?

Have you ever gone on a date with someone, and even though you found him or her to be kind and genuine, you were also able to come up with a whole slew of reasons why you shouldn't go out again? Did you let everything fizzle because of how long the drive would be to this person's place, or because you didn't like how he or she held a fork?

Conversely, have you ever gone on a date in which you two got along so well that it wasn't even a matter of *if* you'd get together again, but *when?* Were you counting down the seconds until your next rendezvous, knowing somewhere inside that your new crush was doing exactly the same thing? If either of these scenarios sounds familiar to you, then you're probably aware of a very simple concept related to dating: Sometimes you have chemistry with someone, and sometimes you don't. End of story.

The fifth and final element of the Adventure in Everything system is *great companionship.* The entirety of this concept can be summed up quite simply: when building and maintaining our relationships with others as we pursue our endeavors, sometimes we are simpatico, and sometimes we aren't. In other words, when we have great chemistry with certain individuals, they are, or have the potential to be, our great companions.

If there are many people in your life with whom you have chemistry, then you probably don't even need to read this chapter. This element can't be taught in a book any more than it can be created by those specialized dating websites that claim to have a patented system for finding mates. Sometimes you encounter those you are compatible with, and sometimes you don't.

If you're like most people, though, you'd probably stand to benefit from having a few more individuals in your life who inspire you to reach your potential. Ultimately, they're who your great companions really are: those who challenge you and encourage an authentic exchange of ideas and feelings. Until the moment that Ronnie approached the CAF booth, he was a kid who'd made a brave decision to have his leg amputated, but he had little idea of how to relate to, or even find, those who were willing to support him. Kelly and Lew not only planted the idea in Ronnie's head that he had the ability to be an athlete, they gave him the opportunity to travel and engage others who had the knowledge to help him accomplish his goals. They became only two examples of the many great companions Ronnie would ultimately have.

Great companions can be family members and friends who play a purely peripheral role in the endeavors we pursue, or they can be those with whom we actually share responsibilities in achieving these goals, such as business associates and creative collaborators. Without the enrichment that these positive relationships provide, it's nearly impossible to both go after our highest endeavors and enjoy the sense of fulfillment that accompanies such an undertaking. Given this, the fifth and final element of the Adventure in Everything system is the most important.

The remainder of this chapter will show you how to find more great companions, as well as provide methods for cultivating and developing the relationships you've already formed.

> *On paper, satisfying relationships are easy to understand and make sense of. In reality, it can be difficult to make them happen.*

How Do We Find Great Companions?

We often hear stories of bands that formed way back when because a couple of brothers were joined by a neighbor or two and began making music together in a garage. Sometimes we find people whom we can collaborate and exchange ideas with or be mentored by simply because circumstances present themselves and we take advantage of our good fortune. What's more likely, though, is that we set out to forge productive relationships by taking a series of actions to make this happen—much like Ronnie did when he began to work with CAF and decided to participate in the Extremity Games.

Whether you're seeking the companionship of peers who have compatible interests and goals, or you require someone with more experience and knowledge who can provide guidance, the next sections will guide you in attracting the right individuals as you pursue your endeavors.

Finding Peers

Even if you don't happen to have a neighbor who can really jam on the guitar, you can still find individuals who are on your wavelength. The types of peers you're looking for, as well as the places you'll find them, will vary depending on the nature of your desires. If you really want to start a band, then finding members could be as simple as posting an ad on Craigslist and trying out whoever responds. Generally, though, you may need to use more creative ways to make connections.

The first step in finding great companions is to determine what qualities you're looking for in other people. Given that a message of this book is to pursue high endeavors with uncertain outcomes, it's likely that the various individuals whom you're attempting to find will share a willingness to entertain ideas that are "bigger" than where they currently are. Returning to the rubber-band metaphor from Element #1, they'll be able to place the second post even farther away from the first one in order to stretch the rubber band. Perhaps they've stepped out of their comfort zone and pushed themselves to define their lives on new and different terms; or maybe they haven't done so just yet but have already identified this as a goal they're currently working toward. Regardless, you'll likely benefit from associating with people who have expressed a desire to seek adventure in their own way.

If you're searching for individuals with whom to develop professional interests, such as business partners or colleagues, it will be advantageous to locate those who possess skills and abilities that complement your own. For example, you might be a big-picture kind of person with a good head for strategy, so you'd do well to find someone who can take care of the details and execute the plan you've put together. To discover prospective partners with similar professional ambitions, begin attending conferences, meetings, and gatherings that are administered by associations related to your industry. Additionally, read trade magazines that feature stories about people with similar goals to your own, review websites that match vendors and employers together, and even comb the classifieds to find anyone who's offering the kind of services that may fit your vision.

If you're attempting to attract creative collaboration, such as someone to animate the cartoon characters you've designed, a co-writer for developing stories, or a drummer to make music with, for example, then you can still pursue the more traditional routes described in the above paragraph, but you may also be well served to try more inventive ways to put yourself out there. Identify opportunities to present or perform your own work, such as open-mike nights and public readings, and pay attention to the other people who also put their talents on display. If certain individuals strike you as particularly inspiring, engage them in a conversation and see if what they have to say is as innovative as their craft. If so, exchange information and go from there.

Other ways to find creative counterparts include volunteering at a not-for-profit organization that makes use of your skills, getting a part-time job in an artistic environment, or advertising your intentions in various venues such as the classifieds.

Searching for individuals who share hobbies and interests should be a fairly manageable process due to the simple fact that our culture is built around bringing people together. If we want to play softball, we can join a league. If we like to play poker, we can start a weekly game with a few friends. If we want to rock climb but need a partner, we can simply go to gyms with rock-climbing walls and meet people there. Given how many activities are designed to be shared with others, foolproof ways of connecting with others abound. Ronnie is a perfect example of someone who took advantage of this. Because he had specific needs, he did well to take a more organized route toward finding like-minded athletes, with the help of CAF and through the Extremity Games.

□ □

Regardless of the endeavors you're pursuing, it's always important to be direct and clear in your intentions when reaching out to others. If you meet people at a conference with whom you feel chemistry, it's not enough just to exchange contact information. Go a step further by writing them, explaining exactly what you want, and asking them if they're interested in connecting. Similarly, if you see someone who inspires your creativity at a café during an open-mike session, sit down with this person and give him or her a clear overview of your objectives in possibly building a relationship.

However you make your approach, always be courteous and respectful of others' time. If you're writing a note, keep it short and concise. If you introduce yourself to someone at an event, offer to buy him or her a drink and use your people skills to show how a connection may be of value to both parties.

No matter what, finding peers with whom you have a satisfying connection will never happen unless you put yourself out there and make your interests known.

Finding a Mentor

In 2009, I purchased a copy of *Inc.* magazine with a very specific goal. This particular issue outlined the *Inc.* 500, which is a list of the 500 fastest-growing private companies in the United States. Then, one by one, I reached out to the CEOs of the various businesses that were highlighted in the magazine and told them about the workshops, seminars, and climbing camps that I was conducting all over the country. My goal was simple:

to forge relationships with people who have demonstrated a deftness for realizing their unique vision. Maybe they'd be willing to pass along their wisdom as to how such success could be emulated. In short, I was seeking mentors.

As I previously mentioned, a mentor is someone who can provide us with guidance as we pursue an endeavor. My friend Geof from the story in the Introduction has been one to me for many years; and I've also established a similar connection with several of the individuals I contacted through my *Inc.* campaign.

The dynamic between mentor and mentee is unique. Mentors aren't just valuable because they assist us in developing ourselves. While in peer relationships—be they romantic, professional, creative, or recreational in nature—each person can make similar contributions to a shared goal, a mentee usually isn't capable of reciprocating in the same way that the mentor is. The mentee's responsibility is to be a good student and then hopefully one day pass along the wisdom he or she has gained, taking on the role of mentor at a later point in time. Given this, good mentors are often hard to come by, since all that's typically in it for them is the satisfaction of helping someone else.

If finding someone to take on this role for you is a strong ambition, commitment and dedication alone won't make this happen; you'll also need to be very clear about the type of guidance you're seeking. To do so, I'd like you to write a letter to an imaginary mentor and explain exactly what you want.

Compose this letter now with the three-paragraph method that you've used throughout this book:

In the **first** paragraph, describe the various ways you've set out to accomplish your goals in the past, such as waiting for opportunities to come to you or psyching yourself out of possible endeavors that seemed too hard to pursue.

In the **second** paragraph, return to the endeavor that you explored in Element #1: High Endeavor. What makes it different from what you've sought out (or, as the case may be, decided not to seek out) in the past?

In the **third** paragraph, reveal exactly what you expect your mentor to do to help you accomplish this goal.

As you might assume, this letter isn't necessarily the ideal way to reach out to someone; this is something that's more for *your* benefit. Actually, I don't even want you to send it to anyone. The point of the exercise is to help you articulate why you'd benefit from some guidance.

□ □

When I contacted all of those CEOs, I can assure you that I didn't use two-thirds of the letter to talk about myself. Instead, I explained how their work was of interest to me. I made them the star by stating that I was interested in learning about what they did. In deciding how you'll reach out to potential mentors, I'd like you to think about the letter you just wrote and establish why such a relationship would be valuable to you. Then draw on that sense of purpose when you initiate a dialogue.

You may do well to contact noteworthy businesspeople who have caught your attention; or attempt to meet potential mentors at trade conferences, workshops, or expos. Regardless of the situation you choose, be sure to communicate your desire to learn more about what they do, and ask as many interesting questions as possible. To borrow a phrase I've heard many people use before, "interested is interesting."

> *Chemistry is easy to spot, but it's far less likely*
> *to be found without putting ourselves into*
> *situations that foster connections with others.*

How Can We Strengthen Our Relationships?

In reading this chapter so far, it's entirely possible that you haven't identified a need to find individuals with whom you'd like to establish a greater sense of companionship. You may already have an abundance of friends, colleagues, and family members, but are you taking advantage of these relationships in every way you can?

As I said at the beginning of Element #5, if you presently have great companions and enjoy wonderful chemistry with everyone in your life, then this chapter probably won't be very useful to you. However, assuming that you're no different from the majority of the people in the world, you'd probably benefit from strengthening even just a few of your relationships so that they're as gratifying as they can possibly be. What follows are five ways to do just that.

1. Be Authentic

This was likely the advice your parents gave you when you went on your very first date in high school. You were to answer your date's questions with as much honesty as possible, and if you didn't feel comfortable doing what he or she wanted during your time together, then you simply had to say so. Being sincere and doing what's true to who you are may be a nice idea—who doesn't want to be accepted as a genuine person?—but that doesn't make it any less difficult or scary to do. After all, what if being your authentic self isn't good enough and causes your connection with someone to crumble?

As frightening as it may have seemed both as a kid and now, being as candid and straightforward as possible about your intentions is going to serve you in the long run. For instance, if you have relationships based on your not being true to who you are, can you honestly say that you're enjoying real chemistry? Forming and maintaining connections through honorable feelings and actions will produce a far more solid foundation than anything built on dishonesty or pretentiousness. When enjoying your companions' company, be as authentic as you can. Everything else will grow from there.

2. Be Specific about What You Want

Specificity is authenticity's close cousin. If you tell some friends that you'd like to see them on a more frequent basis, it might not be enough to just say so. A typical response might be, "Um . . . okay?" The most effective way to reach out to people is to actually invite them to do something, and perhaps create a reason for meeting regularly, such as starting a weekly card game or book club. If you want to see family members more often, you could suggest getting together every Sunday for dinner. By identifying what you want and then being specific in communicating that desire to others, you're doing most of the work; all the other party has to do is answer yes or no.

In more professional settings, it's best to consciously and precisely articulate your needs to colleagues. Whether you're in a meeting, writing a memo, or even just having a casual conversation, being the one who knows what he or she wants *and* is willing to actively go after it will streamline the process of getting things done—and it's likely to earn you some points as well. When communicating with others, always be as specific as possible.

3. Refine How You Give and Receive Feedback

Have you ever expressed yourself in some way—be it through writing, sharing a story, acting in a play, performing in a band, or even just throwing a party—and someone came up to you afterward and said, "That was great! But can I offer you a little . . . constructive criticism?" Did you flinch when they threw in the "But"? Maybe your toes curled downward in your shoes when the person paused before the words *constructive criticism*. Did you ultimately keep a brave and polite face when you received the critique, but then spent the rest of the day forlorn over how nobody has ever liked anything you've done? Even if this particular example doesn't apply to you, you can probably relate to such a scenario when it happens to others. Of course you can, since it's easy to take criticism in a negative way—whether it's constructive or not—and even easier to *give* it in an insensitive way.

What is the ideal way to offer feedback? Well, the best kind is that which is actually requested. Even if you give your opinion with the most sincere intentions—and your comments might be spot-on—if it wasn't wanted to begin with, then you're not likely to make too many friends.

Also, constructive criticism should be exactly that: *constructive*. Telling a friend that his poem is "really good" or "not the best work" doesn't really help at all; it's just assigning a cheap phrase to his efforts and leaving it at that.

If you've been asked to give feedback, you'll need to figure out if this is really what the individual wants. If you do establish that your honest opinion is welcome, avoid simply supplying one or two adjectives, and share your experience instead. Draw the person in by explaining your understanding of what he or she did in order to first establish a common language. Then propose what could have been done differently to enhance your experience, making one or two suggestions as to how this might be accomplished. Each situation is, of course, unique, so it will be up to you to determine how authentic this exchange should be.

When you receive feedback—especially when you haven't asked for it—it's important to remember that most people who offer it have positive intentions and are probably just looking for a chance to connect to you or your work in a meaningful way. If individuals provide criticism that isn't helpful, it's important to simply thank them for their input and move on. If it is beneficial, then thank the stars that you've made acquaintances who know what they're talking about. Perhaps it's time to have tea with them and ask for their opinion on your job, your grocery list, and everything else.

Just kidding. Kind of.

4. Allow Shifts in Your Relationships to Happen

A woman once came to one of my workshops because she found herself in a cycle of depression and couldn't drop the excess pounds she so desperately needed to. After taking some time to discuss her lifestyle, I realized that it didn't lend itself to losing weight. The people she spent time with had been her friends since college, and they liked to eat at restaurants with menus comprised almost entirely of fried foods. Not only that, but no one in this group was ever up for any sort of activity requiring physical exertion.

As you might imagine, recognizing that her oldest relationships were antithetical to her goal of losing weight shook her up a bit. In response, the woman talked to her friends about this, and they got upset and defensive. Despite the possibility of having to spend more time by herself, she decided to distance herself from them. When I last heard from her, she had gotten married, lost a lot of weight, and been maintaining a much healthier lifestyle.

Sometimes you might maintain certain relationships because you feel that you're supposed to: friends from high school, pals from college, or co-workers you go to happy hour with. But would you hang out with them if you weren't forced to see them from Monday to Friday, for instance?

One of the most significant lessons here is to realize that the qualities you seek in your relationships might not be reflected back to you by everyone in your life. It is possible, after all, for someone to be a great person but not necessarily a great companion for you. The story about the woman from my workshop is an extreme example of when people's relationships aren't serving them, but it represents what can happen if we immerse ourselves in a world that isn't compatible with our goals.

Spend some time determining whether or not your relationships are a reflection of great companionship—in other words, do they both challenge and support you? Given how important this element is, it will be valuable to take a considerable amount of time to write about this topic in a stream-of-consciousness fashion in your journal. Alternatively, discuss your thoughts with those you absolutely know are in your life because this connection fits into the vision you have for yourself. Taking a hard look at your current circumstances doesn't mean that you have to totally remove yourself from them, but you must be willing to shift the nature of your relationships. If done with both sensitivity and conviction, this can be extremely beneficial.

5. Reciprocate Great Companionship

When you read that great companions are people who challenge and support you, you might feel that the message of Element #5 is one-sided. Do sentences like this mean that you're supposed to sustain relationships based entirely on whether or not the other person supports and challenges you, with no consideration for how you treat him or her in return?

This, of course, is not the case at all. In fact, if we want to foster more authentic companionship in our lives, and if we really want to enjoy the fruits of our highest endeavors, we absolutely must challenge and support those around us as much as we possibly can. If a friend sets aside half an hour to help us write a cover letter for a résumé we're sending to a prospective employer, then we in turn would do well to spend half a *day* helping him or her do the same.

Ronnie Dickson started out as the beneficiary of numerous resources, including a clinic that helped him become more competent in the use of various prosthetic technologies. In very little time, he went from beneficiary to benefactor by becoming an employee at the clinic.

Perhaps the most effective way to foster greater and more satisfying relationships is to simply treat people as we'd like to be treated.

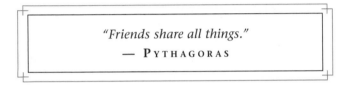

"Friends share all things."
— **PYTHAGORAS**

Had Ronnie never walked up to the CAF booth, signed up for the Extremity Games, and traveled across the country to meet people who were developing cutting-edge prosthetic technology, he would have probably done okay. Given his decision to have his leg amputated, he already showed strength of character. However, had he not formed these relationships, he might have continued as an English major, failed to see how satisfying it is to connect with a community of like-minded people, and never realized his full potential.

Three months after he graduated from college, Ronnie showed up for his first day of residency at the prosthetics facility. At this job, he found an opportunity to collaborate with all sorts of people who cared as much about this work as he did—those who had the potential to be Ronnie's great companions. Given how his studies, lifestyle, and passions all converged, it would be an understatement to say that he experienced fulfillment and satisfaction as he walked through the door.

In fact, that was one of the proudest moments of his life.

Great-Companionship Task List

- Find conferences, workshops, and other public venues that may present you with the opportunity to open a dialogue with potential peers.

- Write a letter to an imaginary mentor, explaining what you want from the relationship.

- Reach out to potential mentors through whatever communication avenues are available.

- Spend time either writing in a stream-of-consciousness fashion or reaching out to those you trust to begin exploring whether or not your relationships are serving you.

BEGIN YOUR ADVENTURE

Let's say that with the help of Element #1, you've figured out what sort of *high endeavor* you'd like to pursue. Inspired by Element #2, you're now able to embrace the *uncertain outcome* that going after it will yield. You've solidified your *total commitment* to accomplishing this goal, after reading about Element #3. You've developed a higher *tolerance for adversity* by using the tools and exercises based on Element #4. And you now have a whole committee of *great companions* with whom to share your experiences, because of Element #5. You know what you want and how you're going to get it, and are motivated to get started.

If this is true, you really don't need to read on. The only thing left for you to do is *act*. Going on an adventure can be scarier than driving on the side of a mountain without any guardrails; with no sense of support, such a situation can cripple you with fear. If, however, fear is not affecting you, if you had your "Aha!" moment 50 pages ago and everything else is just filler until you get started, then make a plan and start driving.

For most of us, though, those guardrails really come in handy. We might believe that they're what has gotten us up the mountain in the first place, because without them, we would have fallen off the edge. Sometimes we simply want a little guidance when venturing into the unknown so we're not completely frightened out of our minds.

In the spirit of providing you with these "guardrails," this Afterword has two basic purposes: (1) to help you assess your own ability to move forward on the path you've chosen, and (2) to get you behind the wheel with your foot on the gas.

> *How is it serving you to stay where you are:*
> *stuck and not taking risks?*

Complete a Pie Chart

When setting out on any new endeavor, it's helpful to have a sense of your resources. For example, if you'd like to begin an exercise routine, you'll need to make sure that you have the time, motivation, and equipment to do so. If you decide to travel to a foreign country, it's necessary to have the financial means, a sense of where to go when you arrive, and, if you don't speak the language, a basic understanding of some key phrases. The same also holds true for seeking to fulfill any pursuit based on the application of the Adventure in Everything system. Rather than a treadmill or phrase book, though, you need the ability to apply the Five Elements of Adventure.

To determine how capable you are of doing so, I'd like you to complete a self-assessment exercise. First, take a look at past endeavors that fell short of your expectations. Perhaps you started a business but it never got off the ground; you tried to raise money for a cause you believed in but never came close to reaching your target amount; or you attempted to take up a new hobby but your interest fizzled out. Write down whatever you can think of in your journal.

Next, draw a circle for each endeavor, dividing it into five sections so it has five equal-sized pieces of pie.

Then make concentric rings inside the circles so they look like targets. Along the outside perimeter of the circles, label each piece of pie with one of the five elements (*HE: high endeavor, UO: uncertain outcome, TC: total commitment, TA: tolerance for adversity,* and *GC: great companionship*). Your pie charts should look like this:

Business　　　　**Fund-raising**　　　　**Surfing**

Now consider these unsuccessful undertakings as they relate to what you've learned about the five elements. Which elements seemed lacking, or even non-existent? When you started your business, did you find that while it was a particularly high endeavor, the uncertainty of your success hindered your ability to take risks? When you tried to raise money for a cause, did you have a total commitment to completing a variety of tasks on a day-to-day basis but beat yourself up for not having what it took to work through adverse situations?

When you attempted to take up surfing, did you simply lose interest because you didn't have any companions to get out on the water with when the waves were good?

Next, fill in a percentage of each area as it relates to how well or poorly you applied the respective element. Use the rings to be as precise as possible in properly representing to what extent you applied yourself. As an example, take a look at the chart below:

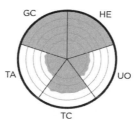

Let's say that I filled in this chart to analyze my goal of starting a business. First, it reveals that I felt this task was the highest possible endeavor. However, I could only fill in one-third of the uncertain-outcome piece, meaning that I had a significant fear of the unknown. Only two-thirds of the total-commitment section is shaded, which shows that while I was focused on accomplishing my goal, there was room for improvement in this category. And the fact that I only colored in one-third of the tolerance-for-adversity segment indicates that I was willing to give up when things got tough. Since I completely filled in the great-companionship piece, I had the support, and even participation, of my friends and family members.

Once you've completed your pie charts, take a closer look at them. What do you see? Do you find that the same elements in different goals aren't filled in equally? Are there any other patterns that have emerged? The basic objective when seeking more adventure in your life is to successfully apply *all* the elements to *all* your endeavors. When this happens, every piece of the pie will be totally colored in—your pie will be perfectly balanced.

Since this is the first time you're doing this activity, your charts won't have all elements totally shaded in. Therefore, I've included the following questions to help you see which areas need work. Take some time to answer them in your journal.

- Is there one (or more) element that's consistently not colored in?

- Consider the element(s) that isn't filled in. Why do you feel that it was a challenge to put it into practice?

- Refer back to the chapter where this particular element was covered in the book and review the exercises there. How could you then incorporate this element into the endeavor you imagined for yourself in Element #1?

In creating these pie charts, you've provided yourself with a way to relate to your goals when taking the next step. By identifying the specific elements of the Adventure in Everything system, you've begun to build the guardrails that will protect you as you move forward.

But what happens when you encounter significant obstacles, such as taking a significant loss for the first year of your new business or not getting people on board to support your cause? If you feel you've come up against insurmountable challenges to the extent that you want to give up, then it's time to take out your journal again and draw another pie chart. This time, fill in the five sections based on how you've conducted yourself so far in this particular endeavor. Have you totally committed yourself to creating success? Have you included your companions in a productive and stimulating way? If you're really struggling, then it's likely that at least one of these elements will be a source of frustration. When you identify these problem areas, your task is to go back and reread the corresponding sections. In addition, apply the specific exercises I've provided for each element to what you're dealing with.

Regardless of whether you're preparing to embark on your endeavor or are already six months into your pursuit, it's always valuable to check in and determine how well you're utilizing the five elements. As I've already said, this type of self-assessment will provide you with a way to remain on track as you move forward. In the next section, we'll explore how to maintain the necessary determination to make your adventure happen.

> *Finding Adventure in Everything is one part planning, one part taking action. People don't want to plan forever, nor do they want to take action blindly. The goal is to find a balance.*

Cristy and the Two Stepping-Stones Toward Adventure

Cristy was still in college when she had the idea to put herself in a scary situation. Although her course work was challenging and she'd had her share of ups and downs, as many students do, her relatively sheltered upbringing in a typical suburban neighborhood meant that there had been few opportunities for her to get out of her comfort zone.

Right before the summer between freshman and sophomore year, Cristy devised a plan. She'd heard about a program that educated participants about the outdoors and required them to survive in specific situations using whatever skills their guide taught them. The promise was that in coping with the stresses of nature, individuals would develop greater interpersonal skills and cultivate a sense of growth within themselves.

Cristy decided to spend part of her break taking part in this program, along with nine other people and the instructor. Their journey took place in the San Juan Mountains in Colorado, and they set out on the first day, not to return for a month. While the other participants all seemed to possess varying degrees of ruggedness, toughness, and resilience, Cristy immediately felt as if she didn't belong. They were all there to trek through the wilderness and survive on nothing but berries, but *her* goal was to escape from a split-level house and not cry for the entire month.

Cristy got on okay at first. She learned about rock climbing, did her best to keep up on the hikes, and followed along when the instructor taught the group new and different activities. Eventually, however, each person was assigned a few days of "going solo." Like everyone else, Cristy was expected to make it in the wilderness all by herself. When it was her turn, she was dropped off in the middle of nowhere, left with nothing but some water and a sleeping bag. Her challenge was to rely only on her wits to survive—with a side order of whatever bugs she could dig up. Somehow, she made it through. Somehow, she was able to tap into her own personal resources and come out on the other end knowing that she had what it took to make it through a difficult situation by herself.

Around the time she got back to the group, rain began to pour continuously. Soaked to the bone and unable to get warm for more than four days, Cristy succumbed to the isolation, the weather, and the fact that she was stuck in the wilderness with a rough-and-tumble crew. She reached the end of her rope.

Their task for that particular day was to climb to the summit of a rugged peak. To lighten their load and get to the top faster, they left their equipment at the bottom. Since it was getting dark, the group only had two hours to complete the hike, but about halfway up Cristy suddenly broke down and went from the girl who was trying *not* to cry to the girl who was actually crying. She declared that she was tired and wet and just wanted to go home. To her surprise, though, rather than dismiss, ignore, or even torment her, the others rallied around her and provided invaluable support. They told her how she totally had it in her to keep going and continued to heap words of encouragement on her all the way to the top.

The other participants' message was that they were all in this together, and as the group made it through the rest of the month, they came to epitomize the qualities that the program had promised to bring out in each individual. And as you'll see, Cristy was no exception.

After college, she had gotten married and opened a small catering company. Once she put herself in what she'd originally considered to be a scary situation— surviving on her own in the wilderness for several days—and allowed herself to be vulnerable, she realized how much she was capable of. She came to trust that the worst-case scenario of being completely on her own was totally manageable. With her business, Cristy enjoyed modest success for several years. She eventually put more focus on raising her children, but her professional endeavors served the larger purpose of revealing how important it was for her to work in an entrepreneurial capacity. While it was possible that she could continue trying to grow her company, she was craving something more. In other words, catering wasn't a scary situation in the least.

In 2002, Cristy was on her way to a dinner party, dreading the same old small talk that she'd experienced at so many of these events. Why was she even going at all? It wasn't like she truly enjoyed being asked where she lived, how long she'd been there, and what her job was. Wouldn't it be better if there was a way for people to feel safe delving into more meaningful conversations? Suddenly, she had a thought: what if, upon entering a party, guests were given a series of questions that weren't considered too invasive or personal?

By the time Cristy had arrived at her destination, the idea had developed further. What if there was an elegant collection of cards for guests to pick from? And instead of asking where the person across the table lived, he or she could ask things like: "What would you do if you could do anything with no risk involved?" "Where would you go if you had to leave the country?" or "Have you ever gone on an expedition into the wilderness and spent the whole time trying not to cry?"

This one night led Cristy to invent a product known as TableTopics, and by 2004 she'd started a company around it. While catering kept her safely in her comfort zone, TableTopics forced her completely out of it. With this new company, she'd had to construct a business plan that allowed for national distribution. To be able to mass-produce the product, she and her husband had to invest a five-figure sum of money just to create a mold for the cards' casings that was elegant enough to fit in on a dinner table amid fine china and wineglasses. In order to make something that appealed to people all across the country, she'd had to fund research, development, and myriad other areas in order to get things off the ground.

This was very much a fearful situation for Cristy to venture into, but she did it anyway. After all, she saw it as an opportunity to foster the love for entrepreneurship she'd developed while running the catering company. It also forced her to draw upon the sense of self-reliance she'd developed from knowing that the worst-case scenario—to be completely on her own in the wilderness without any support—was something she could survive all the same.

When I began reaching out to the CEOs featured on *Inc.* magazine's list of the 500 fastest-growing privately owned businesses, I noticed that coming in at number 364 was a small company of five employees founded in 2004. In 2005, the company's revenue was $389,719. By 2008, it had grown 688 percent to $3.1 million. If you're ever dreading the tedium of dinner-party conversation at an upcoming event, the company's CEO and a new acquaintance of mine, one Ms. Cristy Clarke, has a product you might like.

> *Stepping-stones help us develop our self-confidence*
> *and guide us toward taking calculated risks.*

Cristy is by no means the first person to ever have an idea and then find success in the business world by marketing and selling a product to people across the country. In fact, turning a thought into a prosperous reality embodies the very spirit on which the U.S. was founded. What's most significant about this story, though, is that Cristy wasn't born with the capacity to take great risks and make all her dreams come true. She'd had to work herself up to this type of endeavor, and did so in very specific ways.

Would she have been likely to make the necessary investment to get TableTopics off the ground if she hadn't honed that sense of self-reliance out in the wilderness all those years ago? Would she have known that she wanted to go into business for herself if she hadn't whetted her appetite for entrepreneurialism with her catering company?

While there are countless stories of whiz kids who have started companies like Google and Facebook as college students, most of us are like Cristy in that we need to give ourselves a bit of a boost before we're able to have lives filled with adventure.

Next, I've provided you with two stepping-stones that will better prepare you to incorporate the Five Elements of Adventure into your life.

Create a Mini-Adventure

The month that Cristy spent in the outdoors touched upon all five elements of adventure: she set out to spend this month away in order to challenge herself and develop a greater sense of self-reliance *(high endeavor)*, had no idea if she'd be able to manage the hardships that she'd encounter *(uncertain outcome)*, was forced to reckon with nature all on her own for several days *(total commitment)*, worked past the discomfort and misery that stemmed from the seemingly never-ending cold and rain *(tolerance for adversity)*, and enjoyed the encouragement of her fellow participants while she also supported them *(great companionship)*.

Any true adventure will likewise require the inclusion of all five elements. Even if the one you envision for yourself isn't worthy of making it into an issue of *National Geographic,* it doesn't mean that you wouldn't stand to benefit from the application of the five elements in your everyday life. Cristy didn't spend a month in the wilderness because she wanted to become a park ranger—she did so because she thought it would give her a boost in learning more about herself and redefining the parameters of her comfort zone.

You might decide that you want to start a business, go back to school, or take up a hobby that's typically pursued by people who are younger and fitter than you are. One way to start training yourself to pursue your highest endeavor is to take a mini-adventure in a controlled setting for a specific period of time. My own company, Inner Passage, offers a variety of workshops and camps that concentrate a series of experiences into a fixed amount of time to help unravel all sorts of fears that may impede your ability to take the plunge into the unknown.

Other ideas for mini-adventures could include:

- Participating in an outdoor excursion with an organization that specializes in wilderness survival, such as Cristy did.

- Spending one week (or several) volunteering for a service organization either domestically or abroad.

- Pledging yourself to a charitable event, such as a marathon or walk, that requires you to raise money, train, and travel.

- Taking part in a workshop that fosters personal growth and/or promotes new and different activities.

- Going on a safari.

- Participating in a writers' workshop at a colony or artist community.

- Taking a week off from work and designing a specific and intense volunteer opportunity for yourself, perhaps working in an environment that will be challenging for you. For instance, donate your time to a hospital, assisted-living community, or homeless shelter.

The recurring theme of all these mini-adventures is that they require you to leave your comfort zone and do something you probably wouldn't do otherwise. So when you set out to try an activity with the intention of growing from the experience, it helps to have some sort of structure and support in order to work past the issues that arise.

If you don't feel ready to pursue your high endeavor, then shape your next vacation around one of the above activities or whatever else will challenge you in pro- ductive ways. In your journal, write down how this mini-adventure will incorporate all of the Five Elements of Adventure. If you feel it would be an appropriate step, commit to one mini-adventure within three months of finishing this book. Then set a reminder for two months from now to check your progress and ensure that you've made the proper arrangements to reach this goal.

Take a Smaller Step Toward Your Goal

Cristy didn't just finish college and then throw herself into a large undertaking that demanded months, or even years, of planning as well as an investment of tens of thousands of dollars. When she decided to go into business for herself, she started much smaller and only served local clients. Although she did need to invest capital to get the company off the ground, it was ultimately a safe venture that didn't require too much risk. What it did do, though, was teach her that not only was it something she enjoyed, but something she could prosper from. By starting off with a catering business and sustaining success for ten years, she was able to take a small step toward achieving her objective of creating a product that served a national market.

This part of Cristy's story is a fine demonstration of how valuable it can be to work toward a scaled-back version of your ultimate goal as a trial run. Maybe you want to own your own bookstore and café but first decide to develop a presence as a used bookseller on Amazon to see if you find this type of work stimulating. Perhaps you want to one day qualify to run the Boston Marathon but start by running 10K races instead, working your way up from there. It could be that you've always loved travel and photography and want nothing more than to be a photojournalist, but you gain experience by shooting special events and other subjects. Regardless of the highest form of your endeavor, there is always a simpler, more accessible version that may serve you in solidifying both your interest and confidence in fulfilling your dream in the most successful way possible.

While pursuing a scaled-back variation on your high endeavor might be more easily attainable, it can be a challenge just determining what form it will actually take. In order to help you determine what a good stepping-stone toward your objective is, I have provided a few questions for you to answer in your journal:

- If your endeavor requires a significant investment, such as opening a store or developing prototypes, is there a way for you to use a small percentage of that money to accomplish a single step toward the larger goal, with the option to raise capital or take out a loan if all goes well?

- If you've created a product that you'd like to sell, are there ways of introducing it to the marketplace via the Internet on websites such as **Etsy.com** and **Amazon.com**?

- If you're looking to publish creative content, are there ways to distribute your work without having to sign a contract with a big company?

- If you think you'd like to try a physically demanding activity—such as rock climbing, surfing, or skydiving—are there beginners' workshops you could attend to see if you want to pursue it further?

- If your endeavor requires you to go back to school and formally learn a new set of skills, could you first take an introductory class to help you determine if such an educational pursuit is viable?

In responding to these questions, you may find that there is a way to leave your comfort zone in a less intimidating way. For example, if you wanted to use the Internet to sell your sculptures, but a certain website provides you with a more accessible opportunity to sell jewelry, maybe you start by making earrings, bracelets, and necklaces. So even though your main goal isn't to make jewelry, if you treat each piece as if it were a miniature sculpture, you'll gain valuable experience in how to make your creative output profitable. If you find some measure of success, you could then draw upon it to be more competent in selling your sculptures: you'd be more savvy in terms of the latest trends, you'd be better versed in communicating the value of your work to others, you'd have a greater sense of where and how to find materials, and, most significant, your flexibility about what you sell would spark your overall creativity.

Taking a small step toward your goal is exactly that: a step. If you have a firm idea of what you'd like to do but don't feel you're quite ready to actually do it, spend some time with your journal figuring out why a smaller but related goal might be more attainable. This won't make your high endeavor any less "high," but instead, all the more possible.

Once you've determined what this initial step may be, write down a plan for what you must accomplish and a schedule for how long it should take. Make sure that your first act requires you to complete it within a month of finishing this book.

> *"Why not go out on a limb? Isn't that*
> *where the fruit is?"*
> — FRANK SCULLY

Begin Your Adventure

You are now about to finish reading this book. You may decide to read it again or look for other books with a similar message and read them as well. If you were to do so with as much fastidiousness and commitment as possible, memorizing every word on every page, and as a result could recite any number of theories or concepts that the authors provided, you would have retained a lot of information, have a number of ideas floating around in your head, and be the owner of a nice book collection that you could admire on the shelf.

And you would also have the same life you had when you first started reading.

Or . . . you could own the business you have always wanted, learn a trade you never had the courage to focus on when you were younger, travel around the world for an entire year, or create sculptures or compose music. You could do all of these things because, quite simply, when you finish this Afterword, instead of watching the latest reality show, you could make an inquiry about a business class, trade-school orientation, travel-agent appointment, or art workshop . . . and consciously, deliberately take action.

My conversation with Geof at the bottom of that rock wall in North Cascades National Park all those years ago taught me that I not only didn't want to be a full-time technical writer with good insurance coverage, but that a life in which I didn't challenge myself to find Adventure in Everything wasn't a life worth living at all.

Ask yourself if you want something more for yourself as well. Do you endeavor to attain the highest form of living possible? Do you intend to embrace the unknown? Do you crave a complete and total immersion in the act of pursuing excellence? Do you expect to overcome the obstacles that will inevitably be in your way? Do you yearn for the company of those with whom you want to share joys, struggles, and everything in between?

When you put this book down in several seconds, you will have an opportunity to take your first step. If you do, and continue to take further steps after that, please know that you will then experience the satisfaction that is invariably born of finding Adventure in Everything you do!

□ □ □ □

ACKNOWLEDGMENTS

My deepest gratitude and acknowledgment go to my wife, Elizabeth. Her patience, courage, and vision have supported and helped this project and countless other dreams of mine with compassion, love, and a firm kick in the ass.

To Geof Childs, the finest mentor I could ask for.

To the partners I have shared a rope with: your patience, trust, and willingness to push beyond our preconceived notions of what is possible has left an indelible mark on my soul. A deep bow of gratitude and Namaste to Jon Sargent, Robb McLean, Andy Wise, Scott Smalley, Matt Szundy, Seth Dee, Ian Eastman, and Todd Rutledge.

To these wonderful people, for encouragement, support, and thinking bigger about Adventure in Everything than I could at times: Erica Bennett, Michael Tompkins, Michael Port, Neil Gordon, Steve Benson,

Aaron Benson, Merrill Shattuck, Jason Tullous, Reid Tracy, and Phil Rossi.

I owe a debt of gratitude to the hundreds of clients I have guided throughout the mountains of the world. Working with you is a gift that has yielded deep repercussions in my life, far beyond the serene moments on a distant summit or a single climbing pitch.

Thanks to my parents, Bill and Pam Walker, and my brother, Chris Walker, to whom I am grateful for laying the foundations of adventure in my life and supporting my dreams and vision.

□ □ □ □

ABOUT THE AUTHOR

Matthew Walker, who received a master's degree in applied behavioral science from Bastyr University in Seattle, Washington, has worked as an outdoor educator and mountain guide for the past two decades. Through his company, Inner Passage, Matt's mission is to teach and facilitate leadership development to individuals and organizations via outdoor adventure, and help people reconnect with their professional and personal potential.

Matt has led expeditions throughout all reaches of the globe; and divides his time between climbing, family, and work—seeking adventure in all. He lives with his wife, daughter, and their canine climbing partner in Tucson, Arizona.

□ □ □ □

NOTES

NOTES

NOTES

NOTES

NOTES

NOTES

NOTES

NOTES

NOTES

We hope you enjoyed this Hay House book. If you'd like to receive our online catalog featuring additional information on Hay House books and products, or if you'd like to find out more about the Hay Foundation, please contact:

Hay House, Inc., P.O. Box 5100, Carlsbad, CA 92018-5100
(760) 431-7695 or (800) 654-5126
(760) 431-6948 (fax) or (800) 650-5115 (fax)
www.hayhouse.com® • **www.hayfoundation.org**

□ □

Published and distributed in Australia by: Hay House Australia Pty. Ltd., 18/36 Ralph St., Alexandria NSW 2015 *Phone:* 612-9669-4299 *Fax:* 612-9669-4144 • www.hayhouse.com.au

Published and distributed in the United Kingdom by: Hay House UK, Ltd., 292B Kensal Rd., London W10 5BE • *Phone:* 44-20-8962-1230 *Fax:* 44-20-8962-1239 • www.hayhouse.co.uk

Published and distributed in the Republic of South Africa by: Hay House SA (Pty), Ltd., P.O. Box 990, Witkoppen 2068 *Phone/Fax:* 27-11-467-8904 • www.hayhouse.co.za

Published in India by: Hay House Publishers India, Muskaan Complex, Plot No. 3, B-2, Vasant Kunj, New Delhi 110 070 • *Phone:* 91-11-4176-1620 *Fax:* 91-11-4176-1630 • www.hayhouse.co.in

Distributed in Canada by: Raincoast, 9050 Shaughnessy St., Vancouver, B.C. V6P 6E5 • *Phone:* (604) 323-7100 • *Fax:* (604) 323-2600 www.raincoast.com

□ □

Take Your Soul on a Vacation

Visit **www.HealYourLife.com®** to regroup, recharge, and reconnect with your own magnificence.Featuring blogs, mind-body-spirit news, and life-changing wisdom from Louise Hay and friends.

Visit **www.HealYourLife.com** today!